The Mask, the Mirror, and the Illusion

The Mask, the Mirror, and the Illusion

AWAKENING TO THE KNOWLEDGE OF
WHO YOU TRULY ARE

JULIE HUTSLAR

LUMINOUS EPINOIA PRESS

Luminous Epinoia Press
P.O. Box 2547
Sandpoint, ID 83864
© 2008 by Julie Hutslar

Printed in the United States of America

ISBN: 978-0-9753000-0-8

Library of Congress Control Number: 2008928053

Printed on acid free paper

Cover and inside artwork © 2008 by Julie Hutslar
Author's website: www.jrhutslar.com

Publisher's website: www.luminousepinoia.com

To that part of all of us that is the Voice of the Divine Self.

In Appreciation

As with any inspired creation, the creator does not stand alone in effort. There are many who comprise the final product through their inspiration, support, philosophies, physical assistance, collaboration and love. This book is no exception and I wish to thank those whose names are attached to this effort.

Foremost on my list is my constant companion, J, who is the voice of my Divine Self, a teacher and consistently wise counsel, and for whom my gratitude is eternal. I am also very grateful for my husband's unfailing support, constant love and many, many hours of tangible work, detailed scrutiny, double checks and questions which led to the finished product that I am proud to present.

Also C. P. Webster-Scholten must be added to my list of acknowledged collaboration as she provided the editing skills that were celestial. She gently and kindly transformed my lengthy thoughts and verbosity into perfectly selected and greatly honed words from the English language that summed up exactly what I was aiming for. Bonnie Wehle added her forte to the editing, continuity and cohesiveness of the whole project, and for that I am grateful as well.

Many of my friends and clients urged me to completion when I was wrestling with this creation and I sincerely thank you, Em and Ann especially. Besides all the thinkers, philosophers, teachers, guides, poets and artists who have inspired me, I wish to thank those individuals who I have yet to meet but for whom this was written. So many friends, clients, loved ones and soul journeyers are part of this book, through their love, their need, their stories, their choice or their mutual journey.

Thank you all.

Julie Hutslar   April 2008

CONTENTS

"Because we are eternally the essence of our Creator, we are so powerful that whatever we choose to believe must become our experience. The world is simply a mirror for what we see within."

– Dialogue on Awakening

You have two choices: you can stall or you can consciously choose to awaken. It matters not which you choose, because you will eventually wake up from this dream of living in a tangible world of pain and suffering. We all will. To stall only means you take the long path, that's all. The goal of this book is to shorten that path.

The questions that begin your desire to return Home are the *whys*. Why me? Why here? Why now? Why not? These questions are healthy beginnings to a journey of seeking. The only problem with these questions is that the answers do not lie within the dream. You must look outside the dream, or illusion, for real answers. The *whys* can trap your mind in a circle of never-ending questions, answerable only through the logic of a mind inside a dream.

The key then, is to find a way to see what the dream is, and step outside it. The following is a manual for students along this spiritual journey. It contains practical suggestions for change if that is what you need. It also contains philosophies or ideas that may stretch the mind allowing you to perceive your own illusions. Ultimately, you will find that you participated, in an impressively creative way, in manifesting the experience you consider your life and you will also find that you have the power to re-create it. First, you must come to understand who you are and why you are so powerfully creative. By doing this, we are going to dismantle who you are *not*.

If you could eliminate all the traits, habits and programs that are *not* who you are, but only the products of having bought into the dream, then what would be left? The essential you, that which you already are, but do not know. Awakening is simply knowing who you are. So you see, it is going to be much easier than you thought. It is not changing who you are, it is releasing who you are *not*.

Together we are simply going to discover who you *are*.

SECTION ONE

ACKNOWLEDGING THE

ILLUSION

"The journey to God is merely the reawakening of the knowledge of where you are always, and what you are forever. It is a journey without distance to a goal that has never changed."

– A Course in Miracles

1 What do you Fear and Judge?

"Listen."

I stop. It's dead quiet.

"What do you fear?"

I'm thinking, searching, feeling, and processing. I don't exactly know what I fear.

"Do you fear bears, cougars, mountain lions, or badgers?"

"No."

"Why not?"

"I know they won't hurt me, they aren't part of my life."

"Do you fear money? Do you fear one dollar bills or hundred dollar bills?"

"No."

"Do you fear losing your house? Losing your husband? Living in poverty?"

"No."

"Then *what is it you fear*? What is it that you presently fear that is creating your current condition of unease and lack of peace?"

As you answer that question, you are traveling upstream in your mind until you locate a reservoir of fear. It is a reservoir that only becomes recognizable with your conscious attention and you recognize it as something other than you and identifiable as a unique energy unit. Ask yourself that question right now; better yet, answer it. What do you fear? Right now, in your present state of life, what do you fear? When you identify it, your body validator will go off, which means you might become emotional, tears might well up, you might get goose bumps, or you might have some uniquely identifiable reaction you've felt many times in your life. You will recognize it as something that has been sabotaging your present happiness, and it will probably come as a slight surprise to you.

Identifying a fear is the same as getting an eyelash out of your eye, or removing a sliver from your finger. Once the irritant is gone, everything feels so smooth, but while it is present, it creates a reality that is not what your conscious mind wants. It imputes its own energy into your efforts, into your creative pursuits and into your relationships. How could it do that? Do fears actually exist? What are fears anyway? Can we say they are *real*? Aren't they just mind-created thoughts that carry negative energy? Fears create concern or the strong emotions of dread and panic, so fears are emotional. If you are afraid of a tarantula and your sister is not, who is going to have a rush of panic-induced adrenaline when you encounter one? Your sister may just become focused with curiosity, but why isn't the emotion of fear or panic overwhelming *her*? She remains calm because it is not her fear, it is yours. So if fears are emotional, doesn't it seem like you would have more control over them than you would if they were part of your hard-wired programming or neurology? But as we will see later, maybe all of what we think is our hard-wiring may instead be mind-created thoughts too.

Fear sits at the foot of the King, or the subconscious mind, whispering in his ear what he should do, or think, or how he should respond. But what is your fear and how do you get around it? How do you locate a fear and why is it so important? Fears create your illusion. They sabotage your happiness and your peace, and therefore, they are more important than you can imagine. So let's begin with your fears. Dilly dallying makes no sense if the purpose of this book is to shorten your voyage. Let's get on with it. Bring on the fears!

Notice you may not be able to gain an audience with the King as long as Fear is sitting there imputing its will. There is another way around this though. If you cannot locate your dominant fear by traveling upstream, let's try another route. Look at what you judge and whom you judge? This will be your indicator.

Do you judge people who do nothing for society? Do you judge people who are rich or people who are poor, people who are frugal or those who are generous? Do you judge those who are lazy? What about those who are born with a silver spoon in their mouth? Do you judge people who are overweight, or slow or unintelligent, or have poor oral hygiene? Do you judge those who scam others or who live off someone else? Do you judge people who go to church or people who don't? People who watch TV or people who don't? People who sleep late or get up too early? What do you find that bugs you right now in this list? Let's just jump right in and look at what you may not be willing to openly admit.

If you find you reacted most when you read "people who are overweight," perhaps that is your present focus and are having a difficult time losing weight. What is the fear behind that judgment? Afraid of being overweight? I doubt it. Fear of being undesirable? Fear of being unloved, fear of losing value placed on you through your body, fear of being alone, unloved and unlovable? You will recognize the fear when you see its face. It won't be someone else's fear you see, it will be your own.

What if the statement you reacted to was that you judge people who go to church as people who are being duped, people who are being brainwashed and are unable to think for themselves? Is there a fear upstream somewhere? Do you fear being brainwashed, or losing your uniqueness to a larger whole? Is it a fear of looking for God and not finding anything at all?

What if *all* of those judgments are yours? What if they *all* bug you? Ask yourself this question: Can you find value in anyone or anything? The fear may be that you are not valuable. Or perhaps no matter what you do or who you are, the essence of you is worthless. Therefore everything you see, you judge as not having value. How can it be worth anything when your fear whispers to your subconscious mind, "There is no value here"?

For every judgment, a fear exists. Let's look at the judgments that revolve around people who don't work in a traditional sense for a living, such as homemakers, those on welfare, street people, the independently wealthy, trust fund babies and retirees? The judgment that they are not adding to society or doing anything productive portends a fear upstream. What should their life and how they live it have anything to do with you? Does it offend you? Is it your own fear of being unable to make a living yourself, of being supported? Or do you fear that if you don't work, you have no real value to the rest of us? What happens with these judgments is that, by and large, we don't ever sit down and admit that we have particular biases; so when we fall into one or another of these categories ourselves, we become a victim of our own judgments.

For example, many people, believe that if you don't work, you are valueless. In other words, your work defines you to society. Then, when you retire, after having worked a good long time, you suffer the results of the fear of being valueless. Many people report it as feeling restless, irritable or just unable to find genuine peace.

Do you judge sectors of society as being valueless? The homeless, drunks, drug addicts, criminals? Why should their lives bother you? Why do they offend you, if they do? Is there an inherent fear of being seduced by the dark side, or of being susceptible to addictions of one kind or another?

Do you judge old people as being slow and useless? What about teachers? Do you think they are fit role models for our youth? What about Grandmothers? Teenagers? Lawyers? Medical doctors? Where does the judgment come from?

Do you secretly judge those who are lazy or who use too many resources, or those who squander? Is it your own fear of scarcity, or not having enough? How do these fears color your life? Do you have enough, do you feel fulfilled or completely satisfied or are you always lacking in money, support, love?

What about those who are angry? Do you judge them as being less evolved? What is the fear that would create that judgment? Is there a behavior that dictates your value, and anger says 'less valuable', calm says 'more valuable'? What happens when you scream and yell and shake your children by the shoulders until they cry? Who have you now become, according to the voice whispered to the King? You are the one less valuable now and you need to pay penance with four bushels of guilt. But who made up this mad world? Who is standing judgment on us? It is only us, each of us, and our minds. It's not our conscious minds either, but our unconscious minds, the ones that are always assessing, downloading, processing, analyzing and filing away according to the places *we* put value. Our emotional responses, our strong feelings, our priorities or our lack of responses all play a part in laying down the gridwork of our core beliefs.

Do you judge people who have grease under their fingernails as being less privileged? Or do you believe that those who understand and use astrology are being superstitious? Do you judge others who engage in extramarital affairs as being bad people? Or what about those who lie to their spouses; do you judge them as being evil? What happens then when you lie to your husband or step out on your wife? You fall into a category you have predetermined as being worthy of guilt. Your self-esteem suffers and the mad world continues life after endless life until…?

Do you want to get off this train? Do you even desire peace? That's really all there is, peace or no peace. It's that simple, and your fears hold the answer to finding peace.

What if you have judged those who cannot make their bed every day as being slothful and lazy and those who cannot keep a clean house as being shameful; then the day you fall into depression and are unable to make your bed or clean the dishes, you have just taken a nose dive in self-esteem. You have fallen into your own category of being slothful and shameful. That really helps when you're depressed.

Now let's return to the question, what do you fear? Can you see how you might locate the answer now? Do you see how it might be sabotaging your present life? Ask yourself this: if I were to be completely valuable to God, what would be different about me? Do you see something changing? What do you feel has to be released or added? What part of you needs a makeover? At least in your mind, what do you believe God would find lacking about you? Or try this, on a scale of 0–10, 10 being the highest, how valuable do *you* think God would rate you? Here you are identifying your self-worth, and identifying it helps you discover what core beliefs reside in your kingdom and how they prevent you from experiencing the peace and joy and happiness that you deserve.

Looking at what you judge opens a door to the shadow side of your belief system. If you are ready to release the judgments, simply opening the closet door is enough to allow them to fall out, but if they are still packed up and taped in the back of the shelf, opening the door is only the beginning. Happily, your fears, judgments and values are only related to who you *believe* you are. But who you truly are is rarely related to who you believe you are. So keep in mind, the purpose of this book again is to simply help remind you of what you already know, but forgot, and that is who you *truly* are, which can then supercede who you *think* you are.

The beauty of this is that no matter what you do, or what you say, or whether you choose to do nothing at all, your Divine Self is unaltered. The essence of who you are is unchangeable. It is that which was created by a Divine Creator in its likeness, not failing or sick, weak or limited by time, space and matter, but immortal, eternal, unphased by time, unlimited by matter and able to exist in all space at all times, like its creator. We, each of us, are a unique expression of God-energy. On Earth at this present time, we all agree that diamonds have value. So let's use the analogy of a faceted diamond covered in tar. A diamond's natural qualities are to reflect and magnify light. However, if it is covered with tar, you wouldn't know anything of that hidden trait. Remove the tar and *voila*, the diamond's facets reflect all the colors of the rainbow and are amazingly brilliant. Think of yourself as that diamond, and your fears as the tar. The tar cannot change the nature of the diamond, but it can certainly hide its more divine characteristics.

So essentially, whether or not you uncover the darkness in the closet, locate a fear, work hard on your own self development, it does not change the essence of who you are one iota. So then, why all these questions? The answer has to do with *willingness*.

Willingness is a key to awakening and awakening is what remembering is about. Since we are already Divine, and all we have to do is remember to embody that again, waking up to that reality is all that is required. Unfortunately, the illusion in which we all live is so amazingly convincing that most of us are not willing to wake up simply because we don't know we are asleep. We have no impetus. We believe that the illusion is the world, and we accommodate it unknowingly. So to admit or encourage willingness is to stand up in an illusionary world of sleeping beings. Are you willing to stand up? Are you willing to loosen every fiber that hangs on who you believe you are to become who you already are but are afraid to manifest?

"The master in the art of living makes little distinction between his work and his play, his labor and his leisure, his mind and his body, his information and his recreation, his love and his religion. He hardly knows which is which. He simply pursues his vision of excellence at whatever he does, leaving others to decide whether he is working or playing. To him he's always doing both."

—James A. Michener

2 What do you Value?

After looking at fears and judgments and seeing what you don't want to draw into your life, how do you consciously write the story of your current life the way you'd like? This is where you look at what you *value*. What you value is already establishing your reality. Think of it like this: value can be assessed by time spent with something; thoughts spent on something; mediums of exchange like money spent on something (or someone); or where you choose to locate your body in time and space. For example, if you value a thin and attractive body, but you constantly dwell on the thought that you are fat, guess where your energy value has been placed? More energy is spent on fatness than on thinness and that becomes the value beacon for drawing more of the same to you. Do you value being debt-free? You say you value it, yet, how much time do you spend thinking about how much you owe, thus placing energetic value on having debt? These concepts are not new. I simply introduce them here to help you understand that your thoughts create your world and the amount of time, thought and energy you spend on something dictates the circumstances of your world.

Let's direct this thinking back to peace. Do you value peace? Do you have a bumper sticker that invokes other drivers to be conscious of world peace? In any given day, how much energy would you say you contribute to peace? Do you have five minutes that contain nothing but peace? Yes, I know, too many obstacles arise to limit peace, and, besides, isn't peace something that happens only when you die?

Let me explain here that peace is not just an absence of war, it is a state of being that encompasses a calmness that comes from everything being totally okay. It is a sense of completeness: no need or lack, no trouble or worry, no anxiety or pressure, simply a state where everything in your mind is calm and whole.

I am focusing on peace for two reasons. One is that if peace is the absence of conflict and the presence of calm, relaxed and accepting thoughts or presence of mind, then it is a worthy goal. It allows you to see more clearly, to make decisions coming from a strong centeredness and peace opens a space for feeling the joy that the present moment has to offer. The second reason I am dwelling on peace is because *inside* the illusion, the feeling of peace is the nearest taste of reality we can reach while still in the illusion thus hinting at what is outside this mind-created box. Either way, to use peace as a choice makes it much easier to make decisions and gauge responses.

So, let's say you have located a fear from your questioning in the first chapter. Think of a fear as a bubble of energy containing something dark, and that darkness has power over you because you think it is real. That's really all it is. No matter where it came from, how long you've had it, how real it seems to you, it simply is a bubble of energy with a dark spot in it. When you think of it this way, it doesn't really seem that powerful, does it? If every being alive does not share the same fear, then the fear cannot be real. That means it is mind-created. Thus, it is energy. Energy does not require that you fight it or reason with it; it simply needs to be transformed. Energy never ceases to exist, it just gets re-created or transformed into something new, or it becomes stagnant, which means that it has not moved in a long time. So that is all you are going to do with the fear that you located. You are going to transform it.

And it really isn't about dwelling on the whys and wherefores, but only on the spot of darkness in your energy bubble. Like a spot on a dress, focus on removing the spot, gently, kindly, but with concentration on the goal of no longer having a spot on your good dress. Well, *you* are God's good dress; do you think you are worthy of an unsightly spot?

We are simply going to use light, instead of water or solvent, to remove the spot. When a space is dark, how do you transform it? You turn on the light. It is that simple with a fear. Your first step is to become aware that you have a spot. Someone may point it out to you (Fred, you have some of your lunch on your tie), or you may see it in the mirror (Good grief, I have spilled all over myself), or maybe you don't discover it until you do laundry (How long have I been wearing this blouse looking like that?). Translated into metaphysical terms, that means other people may bring you to your fears by lighting them up or pushing you into them, you may see your fears mirrored in others through watching them react to their fears (which may be yours too), or you can look for them internally with flashlight in hand. I am suggesting the latter. It feels more in control, it is the shortest route and it is time to do it.

Let's start with a real sabotaging fear: the fear of being worthless. You pull it to the surface. You acknowledge, "Yes, I have a fear somewhere deep (or now somewhere on the surface) that if the truth were known would reveal that I am valueless, that my worth to anyone or anything would equal about zero or maybe even negative seven."

There it is. It is an energy bubble with a dark spot on it. It is nothing more than that. And yet, if you were to look at the effects of that dark spot (like a grease spot on your tie), you would see it has kept you out of expensive restaurants, upper crust clubs, speaking circuits, the movies and relationships with others. In other words, it has defined your social situation and it has affected your self-esteem. And this, in turn, defines the rest of your life: what you feel capable of, worthy of, or entitled to. No reason exists to give it any more power as you look at it now. In fact, you are bringing it up to reduce the power it has wielded, and dwelling in sadness over your seemingly lost life only gives it more power. Bring it up and get the laundry spot remover out, or in our case, grab the flashlight and turn it on.

In the case of worthlessness, your flashlight is going to be Truth. Do you believe that a Creator brought about all that currently lives and breathes? Do you believe that Creator creates from infinite power and capability? Do you believe you were created from this creation energy too? If not, what created you? If you are so unique that you were created out of worthless or partial creation energy, wouldn't that make you special in itself? Wouldn't that make you like the mutant gene that creates a four-leaf clover, more prized than the healthy, perfect expression of clover? No, I think you were created by the energy that created all of us, the Source of All. That source does not create anything valueless, and whether or not you believe in an omnipotent being or a peaceful, loving being or a river of life-force, the bottom line is this fact: there is only energy. We are only energy and energy cannot be good or bad; it is simply energy. What you assign to any specific bubble or unit of energy is entirely up to you. Then that energy holds the vibration of what your mind imputed upon it. You cannot be inherently without value, but your energy unit can carry the vibration of worthlessness, which means that you can reassign an energy unit a different vibration. And what is it that is doing the reassigning? It is your mind. That is all. *It is your mind.*

You hold the power then, don't you? All the little energy units that comprise your being have been assigned a vibrational program, and either it works for you, or it is becoming limited and restrictive. So, upgrade your programming. Hold your light (the love in your heart, or the clarity of vision, or the knowledge of truth) and shine it on this spot. See what happens. You could call it a miraculous spot remover. The dark spot simply dissolves and becomes energy awaiting assignment for use as something else. But if you are using any of the above—love, clarity or truth—it has already become reassigned by using the energy you placed on it as a template. The more energy you assign to this task, the greater value you have given it.

So if you have located a dark spot containing dishonor and have removed it with your light wand spot remover, then your life will begin to accommodate this new change in your energy self. Others may try to remember and bring up the old spot, but it only remains in their memory, it is not actually present any longer. In practical terms, you may have to address others honestly when they attempt to dishonor you; you may want to buy yourself nice things honoring yourself in a way you have never done; you may want to do nice things for other people as a way to honor them as you honor yourself. In other words, as you allocate time (either in addressing someone instead of ignoring them, or selecting something new), you will be sending the message of *value* to your whole energy unit. Your energy unit now knows you've put your money where your mouth is, and it obeys.

Keep in mind that value comes from energy spent on something, so whatever *you think* is actually energy being spent. Monitor your thoughts while you are reassigning fear energy. Ask yourself, "Am I replacing it with another fear? Or doubt? Can this concept really be this simple? Will I feel stupid if I do it and nothing happens?" Your thoughts are attempting to reassign the fear energy, and the only judgment is your own. So even though reassigning dark spots of energy can really be quite simple, other components of your makeup introduce ideas that make it seem more difficult.

Several key players travel with you on this journey of awakening, and they include those who will embody the energy of sabotage and those who will encourage and support you along the way. They will also include those who will mirror your fears and those who will help hold the flashlight.

"Until you have become prepared to know Me it is but natural for your personality thus to question and rebel. Once you recognize My Authority, that moment the undermining of the authority of the personality has begun. The days of its dominion are numbered, and you will more and more turn to Me for help and guidance."

— Joseph Benner, The Impersonal Life

3 Meeting the Key Players: The Ego and the Spirit

Before we go any further, it is paramount to introduce and clarify two key players: the Ego and the Spirit.

The Ego

The **ego** is the term used here to indicate that part of you that promotes or encourages *separateness*. It is not necessarily your personality; in fact, the ego is not actually you at all. However, it exists, and only exists because it was thought into existence, not because it was originally created by the Creator. It is much like a thought: it can cause fear as soon as you think it and once you have thought it, it takes on a life of its own. The ego has been thought and now it exists in the minds of all of us as if it were very real, very cautious and very capable. To understand what part of you it is, let me describe what it creates.

Comparing and contrasting your life with others is what the ego does best. Every thought you have that has differences at its core—differences in your body versus hers, your salary versus his, your spiritual evolution versus theirs—are witnesses to the presence of the ego. You could say that if this thought had a goal it would be to keep itself alive. Like any other being, self-preservation is the underlying motivation, and self-preservation keeps the thinkers of this ego (us) from knowing who we truly are. If we did know, as you will come to see, the ego would cease to exist, for there would be no more thoughts of it.

The ego is that part of you that encourages thoughts that produce anxiety, depression, lack of self-worth, anger, frustration and fear. In fact, the ego actually uses fear as an important tool to keep you allowing it to be in control. The ego knows that if it does not promote itself and impose into your world, then it would cease to exist. And truly, if you lived only in the spirit, within the peace of God, it *would* cease to exist. So I guess it produces a genuine fear. You see, the ego is nothing but a big projection, so it is, in fact, *not* real. It is much like the image of the Wizard of Oz projected onto a huge screen by the little man behind the curtain. The Wizard never really existed as everyone thought. But he existed as powerful and scary in the minds of all the people in Oz, because they believed he did and feared him. And because they feared him, they gave him some of their power. So there you have the ego, a pompous, projected image that does not really exist except in our collective minds.

The ego does *not* believe that it does not inherently exist, so it tries to convince you that it is truly *who you are*. How many generations of Munchkins and Oz citizens believed that the great Wizard of Oz clearly existed and based many of their beliefs and actions on his existence? How many millennia have we believed that the ego is who we are?

The ego's logic convinces you that you are your body. This logic is its main tool for inflicting fear and maintaining control. Now you might ask the ego, "Well, if I am my body, what continues after I die?" Does this question ever get answered? Not by the ego, or by those who have no validation of the spirit. Even those who actively *do* believe in a spirit or an afterlife still fall prey to the tactics of the ego. If you truly believed that the Essential You were a spirit, incapable of being changed, destroyed or marred in any way, why would you believe the ego when it tells you that you can be harmed or even die if you do not listen to its wisdom? You would accept that premise because you believe that the **You** in that last sentence is your present body and identity, and that is the thinking that must be challenged.

Choice number one, then, is to understand that we are inherently *not* the ego. Choice number two is to be able to recognize the ego when it interjects itself. Because if you choose to live more fully guided by your spirit self, you must know how and why the ego will try to sabotage you. Choice number three is knowing and accepting that your ego has a motive different from the spirit so you won't beat yourself up when you are unable to make spiritually-based choices. You will simply know you have a worthy opponent.

The ego is more. It is everything that makes you say snide remarks. Now think about it, why does the ego want you to say a snide remark? It separates, remember? It drives you to feel unkind thoughts towards another human being. What happens the moment when all humankind knows we are all made of the same fabric and that it is spirit, not ego? What need for the ego would we have? None. It would cease to exist. It would be a very different world, it would in fact, no longer be Earth, it would be Nirvana, or Enlightenment, or Heaven or whatever you want to call it. Without the ego, there is only love, forgiveness, joy, peace and happiness.

I am sure the ego does not like this spotlight on it anymore than the little man behind the curtain liked Toto pulling the divider back to reveal it was just a small man pretending to generate a great Oz. Nevertheless, this spotlight is necessary, not to begin a fight or even identify an enemy, but to understand, to enlighten, to awaken.

Let's look at the ego that is active in someone's life. Consider the situation of Cynthia. She is at work. She has a co-worker who challenges her, who irritates the heck out of her. Their boss calls Cynthia into her office to be reprimanded; she appears to be in a little trouble. Now, she can either take the criticism like a responsible adult or she can choose to blame someone else. Her mind flickers to her irritating co-worker who, if you really stretched it, could possibly be seen as having a hand in this misdeed. She could simply pull his name into it. Maybe her boss wouldn't go for it, but it could muddy the co-worker's name just by suggesting that the deed was either his idea or he encouraged Cynthia to do it. This example illustrates the voice of the ego. It is trying to make Cynthia look good at the expense of someone else. It is separating; it is bringing malice and negativity to an innocent person. It is maintaining a separation between these two employees, and it wants Cynthia to look good at any cost.

Another example takes place at a family gathering where, during the course of the day, you overhear a relative say something slightly derogatory about you. You choose to be insulted (the ego) and you choose not to speak to this person again as long as she lives (the ego again). You then hear other things from other people that fuel how mean and spiteful this person is to others, which provides reason and rationale to your little war. Though your heart says to forgive her, she is human after all, but you now have said or thought much worse about her, and your ego is firmly entrenched in a stalemate. At this point, the spirit makes its presence known in the option of forgiveness, but the option gets closed off by the ego. Are you beginning to see that you live with the voice of the ego at all times? It even keeps you a slave as illustrated in the two following scenarios.

Let's say you meet someone who is a super person and who treats you beautifully and honorably. The ever present ego senses danger and digs up all those loathsome things about you that you have tried to forget. In fact, it shares them with you in exquisite detail to generate self-loathing just at the right time, so you don't feel worthy of this new person. It directs you to end the relationship before the other party does, because it is just a matter of time before this beloved person finds out what a horrible person you are.

Or when something looks promising in your career or with a desired project, the enslavement continues as the ego whispers the voice of uncertainty, trying to keep you down and manageable; it supplies many reasons why it would never work and, even though it is what you would love to do, why you can never get what you want most. At the base of your self-esteem you will find vestiges of the ego.

The ego is beginning to sound like a dictator, isn't it? As long as you are giving it what it wants, it is happy. But it is insatiable. Just as with external desires that simply lead to another and another, the ego's bottomless appetite continues to be fed.

> *You must have noticed an outstanding characteristic of every end that the ego has accepted as its own. When you have achieved it, it has not satisfied you. This is why the ego is forced to shift from one end to another without ceasing, so that you will continue to hope it can yet offer you something. – A Course in Miracles*

The body is not the ego, but the ego tries to manipulate it. It tries to get you to believe that you are your body; because if you believe this, you have many more fears it can manipulate you with. It can hold out the ultimate fear of death, of old age, of being sick, of hurting, of looking old and not being desirable. If you knew you were inherently *not* your body, but a spirit, what hold would even death have over you? You would say *adios*, nice vehicle, now I'm on to another. The ego does not like this kind of talk. It says, "Look, you *are* your body. Do you *see* a spirit here? NO, so forget this whole spirit business talk and get back in line. Life is suffering. Get used to it!"

Here is a way to determine if the ego is involved. Simply, the ego generates energy that is negative. It separates. It chastises, it criticizes, and it makes you feel low. It generates anger, hatred, opposition, competition, self-loathing, irritation, feelings of superiority and inferiority, anguish and suffering, grief and death. So too does jealousy and greed come from the ego, along with judgment and intolerance. Feelings of being betrayed, abandoned, rejected, all carry the mark of the *Big E*. If you keep this in mind, you can walk through your day and identify every response, every interaction, every thought, every newspaper headline and every feeling that comes from the ego, and those that do not.

The Spirit

Though we hinted at it previously, really what is the *spirit*? It is what the ego is *not*. It is exactly the opposite. It generates love and connectedness, it offers sacredness and honor. It is forgiving, even when it may not feel natural. The spirit is divinity in action if you give it the opportunity to be active in your life. Where there is love, forgiveness, happiness, joy and peace, there is spirit present. When you choose a response that brings you peace and results in communion with another, the spirit was making the decision and directing the efforts at that moment.

The spirit is your divine essence. It exists even when it is not in a manifest vehicle. Your paltry physical body cannot contain it. Your spirit is much grander than a human body. The body is simply the vehicle to express what you came here to express, but the spirit is not contained by that body. Part of it can be present when someone beloved far away is sick or dying. Another part of it can be in another realm, greeting someone who is passing over to another place. Think of it like this, your spirit is that which was created originally by God. Would God create something to express godliness as limiting as a human body: frail, sickly, limited by physical space and time, that decays and dies? Not the Creator of the Universe! From that all-powerful creating, extending energy you would more likely find a being of infinity: eternal, complete, peaceful, loving and unimpeded by walls, time or dimensions. Compared to that, your body alone is extremely limiting.

The spirit is the life-force energy that doctors identify as being alive or dead. The spirit is that which animates all living things. It is the creative life force energy of the universe. It is the fabric that was rolled out and fashioned into souls. It is the thing that connects us all. It is the reason you can read another's mind, the way you can intuit things that don't have to do with you, the way you can feel what someone else is feeling. It is because we are the same stuff, the same essence.

I like to use the analogy of the vehicle. Let's say you, the *real* you, are driving a car. The car is your body. The car does not know the rules of the road, but you do and you brake for red lights and wait for on-coming traffic when you must yield. The car knows none of this. Now the ego is the backseat driver trying to tell you where to go and why, and is insisting that the car is actually *you*. Does that make any sense?

So, it comes down to this simple rule: If something in your world generates love, forgiveness, happiness or peace, the spirit is present in that situation. If it is anything else, the ego is in charge. And keep in mind that the body is an instrument of either one, whichever is in charge. And who runs the show is whoever has the most power. That means that if you allocate personal will or power to the illusory ego, that is who you will be working for.

If you consciously put more and more energy, effort, trust and belief into the nature and existence of the spirit, then that will be your guide. Look at your world and identify your thoughts, your actions, your words; they have an origination. If the thought or deed generates love and joy, it was created from your spirit. If it generates hatred or anger, its creator was the ego.

The purpose of this book is to empower you to live more fully and more richly in your highest, spirit self, bringing the beauty and fulfillment that come from its constant presence in your life. These two all-important players are interwoven throughout the book; this chapter is only their introduction.

It would be accurate to say that the ego is anything that is **not** the peace of God. The spirit is the eternal peace of God.

"The illusion is your miscreation which overlays the reality and the clarity as expressed and extended through the Mind of God. There is nothing but perfection and truth that is resonant in the Mind of God. That which is not seen or recognized as being perfection and truth has been misperceived as an illusion of truth."

— Dialogue on Awakening

4 Reality Versus Illusion

A clarification of the terms reality and illusion are necessary at this point. When I use the term *reality*, I am referring to that which has been created by *real* creation energy. It does not imply a three-dimensional object, something we can touch, see or feel. Such objects are *tangible* or *material*. By real, I mean that it was created originally by an authentic, genuine Source. Using Webster's Dictionary to assist our understanding, reality is "relating to fixed, immovable, permanent things; not artificial, but genuine; fundamental, essential; occurring in fact." So using this definition, it is hard to see how our bodies would fall under this category; they are always under some form of change. One day you can weigh 250 lbs and a year later, having lost 80 lbs you may weigh 170 lbs. Are you then not *real*? And when you die, and your body is either cremated or buried and it decays, what part of that body was essential, and what part was fundamental, genuine, permanent? Where is the genuine article? If it is anywhere with the body, we would cease to exist the moment we stopped breathing long enough to extinguish physical life.

So that begets the question, what then *is* real if it isn't our body or our illusionary world? What is *real* originates only from the hand of the Divine, from the Authentic Source. What is that? It's not your body. Look around your world, perhaps very little is real, given that definition. What is real is that which has its origination in love, which as we have been discussing, is the essence of our Creator and thus ourselves. In Tom and Linda Carpenter's book, *Dialogue on Awakening*, their guide offers a guideline for answering that question. What part of my world, my experiences or my emotions are real?

1. *Is that thing which I am questioning eternal?*
2. *Is it limitless?*
3. *Is it possible for me to experience any aspect of this thing in a way that is not loving?*
4. *In each and every circumstance, is my being resonant with this thing bringing me a sense of absolute peace?*

Experiences and feelings, as well as thoughts, fall under the definition of real, and manifest objects (which certainly aren't eternal or limitless) fall under the category of illusion. Perhaps it is easier to understand what is real if first you understand what an illusion is.

Illusion is that which is "deceiving, misleading, an hallucination, a pattern capable of reversible perspective." This is the term I will employ when talking about mind-created paradigms or, rather, the holograms we create from our egos. Let me explain this concept further. We all believe we are living a *material* or *tangible* reality, one that we have very little ability to adjust or change. We believe that it is how life is and we have come to work within the limitations of it. Everyone sees the world in a different way, or the world has formed itself differently for you than for another, and that world is our personal illusion or hologram. Just like a hologram, it appears three-dimensional, is complete with material manifestations and is as large or small as we have programmed it to be.

For example, I am acquainted with a kind, older couple that has lived their whole life off the land. They are farmers and life has been physically difficult for them in many ways. The area where they have farmed and were born in is flat and wind-beaten with little natural moisture. The trees are short and stunted, reflecting the lack of water and constant wind. One natural blight or another is always wrecking havoc with their crops. It is rare indeed when they reap a full and bountiful harvest. When you look at their physical bodies, you can also see their *illusion* has worn them down as well. The woman is crippled in her bones. She cannot stand straight and has so many ailments she has forgotten the names of them all. Every time a storm moves in, she feels it in every bone in her body, as a warning, and also as pain. The husband is stooped and tired. They live in a run-down shack with no visible beauty anywhere near it. They have fully accepted this world as their own, they don't try to fight it or change it and, strangely, they have an unusually optimistic attitude, given their situation in life.

Now, how do you account for some people's lot in life? Is it determined by a draw of the straws? Destiny? Karma? Or it could simply be that *we believe one thing about ourselves and our Creator believes another.* So since we have the choice to create our own image, we are allowed to live it. And I believe that is exactly what we do. We create, but instead of using creation energy streaming straight from the Divine, the genuine love energy, we use ego-created energy. And that energy actually *does* create, since we are creators ourselves. However, it does not create what I call a growing, self-sustaining, life-giving reality. Instead, this ego-generated energy creates something limited: it is our own personal hologram. Inside this hologram is only what we have programmed at some point, with borders, limitations, restrictions, beauty or not, love or not. But all of it has one thing in common; it is not self-rejuvenating. It is a limited space and eventually one day we run into the edges of this hologram.

So the term *material manifestation* will refer to tangible expressions of co-creation and *reality* will refer to experiences or manifestations that have their roots in the spirit world, that are created from divine creation energy and in which you find love. The word *illusion* will refer to those experiences or manifestations that stem from ego-created energy, and have their source in fear and other expressions of mis-creation.

Creating an Illusion

Illusions are created using fear as a reference point. Whatever mind-created fears plague you, your personal illusion will construct itself to accommodate and compensate for those fears. Unfortunately, most of the fears that create your world are held deep within your subconscious mind, perhaps in response to something that happened before your present conscious mind had any awareness. *A Course in Miracles* says that nothing exists outside you that did not first exist within your mind. The concept of a mind is best defined by Robert Perry for A Course in Miracles. He defines the mind as:

> *The aspect of self that includes the faculties of awareness, volition, thought and emotion. Mind is completely non-physical; it should not be confused with the physical brain. Mind in Heaven is one with Spirit. Mind on earth is separated from its true nature and split between the opposing voices of the ego and the Spirit, requiring it to choose between them.*

Therefore, every person who shows up in our life-drama was hand-picked by the fears of our own mind, or through the love present in our mind. As I discuss below in more detail, the choices of your world stem *only* from either fear or love. Not only is every person, relative, and friend a product of your subconscious thought system, but so is every manifest object as well. Your home, your job, your limitations, your gifts, are all being created as you shift and grow, expand your mind, or release fears. The corollary is that your world will also accommodate new fears and reflect them back to you as the creator.

Have you ever known someone who had a deathly fear of heights? Perhaps this fear prevented them from staying in high rise hotels, from hiking up ridgelines or mountains, from going on cruise liners, from riding in glass elevators, from experiencing Ferris wheels or roller coasters or movies filmed in a helicopter. It may seem insignificant to us, but if it is a real fear (meaning the belief that real dangers are present), it will forestall many plans due to the dread that heights may be encountered. Once this fear is overcome, the world expands and becomes less fearful and more friendly, many more options appear and a greater sense of freedom. So to release a previously held fear is to be awarded a badge of courage and freedom!

Think of the fears that create our manifest experiences, the ones we are unaware of that are founded on our mistaken identity of self. They form a real boundary for us and prevent us from certain experiences just like the fear of heights would do. Ever notice also that those fears that we resist so adamantly continue to plague us? It's as if we are drawing the very thing we are most afraid of into our illusion. In fact, we are. Our world is built on it, and we are going to see it from time to time.

Have you been around someone who is afraid of crowds or of being in public? At first you think it's quite silly, if you do not share the same fear, but after you witness their panic attack and outbreak of sweat and paranoia, you realize they have a serious barrier. Nothing you say or do will convince them to enter a crowded public place. You can then imagine the way this fear would arrange their life differently than yours. They would order their necessities from catalogs or on-line merchants, and her friends would only hang out with them if no one else was around. They could not show up to support friends or family at functions where someone was performing either in music or dance, they would not be part of family holidays without experiencing pain and anxiety. So the feelings others had for them would mirror in many ways the way they think of themselves; a loner, alone, unsupported, misunderstood. Fears create our illusions.

These examples are fairly simple ones that can be witnessed and correlated. The ones that are the most restrictive cannot be seen. They are the ones that keep you small and damage your self-esteem. Think of your sleeping dreams. They are a compilation of many snippets of things you thought, saw, or heard or they are symbolic of some aspect of you as yet unwhole. Your waking dream/illusion is the same. It is compiled of pieces of your desires, your fears, your random thoughts, as well as your subconscious beliefs. Suffice it to say, your illusion was custom-made for you, by you. My goal is not to dwell on how illusions are created, but on how they can be re-created and ultimately dissolved.

Expanding Illusions

Let's consider this concept of a reality that is self-sustaining, has no limitations or borders, but is filled with things that grow and create themselves when the journey calls for expansiveness. This reality is one derived from your authentic creation energy or love, not from the fears and limited vision of the ego.

Using a metaphysical (non-tangible or abstract) experience to illustrate the boundaries of our self-created illusions that then manifest themselves as our present world, let me share a method that frequently presents itself during my healing work. An image is presented to me in the language of the soul, symbolism, for the purpose of healing or transforming. This image often appears as a hologram. What becomes apparent as I reach the boundaries of this hologram is what was programmed, and therefore, what is needed. For example, once while working with a woman, I entered into her hologram through her heart energy and with my mind's eye, I saw a young boy sitting at the end of a long table. There was no one else in the room, no paintings on the walls, no snacks around on credenzas, no plants, only this long table that was austere and formal. I approached the boy and asked him what he was doing there. He said he was waiting to eat; he was waiting for someone to bring him dinner. I asked how long he had been there and he replied it had been a very long time. My job as facilitator of this healing work is to understand what my client needs to guide her to her highest self. So I asked the boy, as he was symbolically guiding us, what he needed. It was obvious, his reply was, "dinner." In looking through the lens of symbolism and the subject of the energetic heart, it felt obvious also that what my client needed was nourishment in the heart area, or relationships that provided sustenance.

What then has to happen is that the limitations of the hologram must be replaced, not with another hologram that is larger, full of all kinds of food items, but a reality that contains a food source that does not depend on someone else bringing food. It needs a self-sustaining energy source, like solar energy with the sun never going behind a cloud.

Experiencing someone's metaphysical hologram is essentially hearing the voice of the spirit spoken in concepts, images and symbols as opposed to languages. You have a visceral sense of the energy of things without words, metaphysically. I'll be wandering over a mountain behind a stream and then, just like that, nothing. No sky, no sun, no thing, only the end of things. There is simply a void. It's not dark, it's more like being inside a cloud, where you can't see a thing, no sense of perspective or anything. Then I know I am at the end of the ego's programming, and I know what we have to work with is only contained within this hologram. But I also know that my client is unhappy with their world, or we wouldn't be working together. They usually have reached a place where the limitations they feel are starting to be painful and no longer fit their new desires.

You know that you have reached the borders of your hologram when you desire something, but do not already have it. If it were in your programmed illusion, or hologram, you would already have it. If it does not exist in there, it certainly feels like persecution as you try all kinds of things to obtain it, but still do not get it. The key then is either to expand the hologram, eliminate the hologram altogether, or create steps that allow this thing you want to enter your illusion. Your hologram is simply your own personal illusion, whereas the term *illusion* applies to our collective mind-created, world experience.

This is the time when the opportunity comes to expand your personal illusion. It is the time you update your programming, and it is very simple. Actually, you do it all the time, but may give up before programming is complete. You want something that isn't inside your hologram. Whether it is a person, place or thing, you desire something that you cannot manifest. What you are doing is imagining something out there in the void. You can imagine it clearly, but there is no pathway as yet from it to you. It is floating around in the clouds just outside your holographic walls. A pathway will form if you simply continue to image this desire with clarity and focus, wholly intent upon having this missing thing. The key here is that the love of the thing or the desired experience can create a pathway of a different kind. Love will create your reality, as opposed to another illusion or hologram based upon fear.

That is one explanation for manifesting your own reality. And it explains why it doesn't often happen overnight. If you had unwavering faith, it could happen in one instant. If you are working to build that faith, it may take a little longer. But if you can imagine that you are growing a path to lead this beloved experience or person or object into your life, you could also be more patient and your faith could grow too.

The key is that you imagine what you want, wish and desire, what is it you'd love? Then, think expansively and be creative as you welcome this energy. When you think of this desire simply as another form of energy, it becomes easier to draw it to you versus the thought of some heavy, expensive or otherwise limiting tangibility that keeps you resisting it.

You don't want to replace one hologram with another, because a hologram will always be limiting, maybe not now, but eventually. You want to create with self-sustaining energy that comes with its own energy source, its own source of nourishment and never is depleted. This is divine creation energy. Ask yourself the question, "What is my motivation for wanting this thing?" Is a fear present (lack, perceived value, loneliness) or is your motivation based on love (joy, happiness, connecting)? You don't want to draw the energy of *wanting* to you which is what happens when you simply want and want. When you fixate on the desire for a person or thing, what you are actually doing is sending the beacon of desire, and what you receive in return is that thirsty feeling of desire, but not fulfillment. To find or draw something into your hologram, you must first imagine or feel fulfilled as if it were already present. Then your mind fills in the details of this desire drawing it to you because like attracts like. It is already there in your imagined mind. Create your world with what you want, trust that it is there before you actually see it with your physical eyes, and in confidence expect that because you know who you are you can call upon it and create it.

Identifying Ego Illusion Markers

Next we must identify that which exposes the ego world. The ego world is one big blur; it all looks the same, and it all feels real. It is unquestionably concrete. Analyzing the word *concrete*, we learn that it comes from the Greek words *con* meaning "with" and *creed* meaning "belief." The word that epitomizes the material world, "concrete" takes its meaning from "with belief." Yet, belief seems like the opposite of material. Could it be that our beliefs validate or make something concrete for us? Just that bit of etymology will shake the ego world a little, but let's return to identifying the ego world. Salvador Dali created a painting entitled, *Dali at the Age of Six When He Believed Himself to be a Young Girl, Lifting the Skin of the Water to Observe a Dog Sleeping in the Shadow of the Sea.* Perfectly titled, the painting matches its description and that is what we are going to do with the ego world, or illusion.

We're going to set your mind with a task of identifying anything that represents the ego world, anything that is a front for reality. Whether you do this intentionally or not is up to you, but simply reading this section will clue the mind into the search. Remember the ego's job is to provide a convincing reality that keeps us plugged into it. Once we begin to question its structure, life as you know it will never be the same.

Let's set up the search criterion: the world of the ego is illusionary. We begin by looking for anything that does not make sense, and that means little things as well as big ones. Why do we kill other people to maintain peace? Why do we argue to get along? Why do we spank our children to keep them safe? Why must we fear a god that supposedly loves us? Why do we invest so little in teachers, who are the models of the very citizens who will form our future, yet pay so much to actors who entertain us for 90 minutes? Why are we punished for telling the truth and rewarded for keeping quiet? And why does no one answer these questions and rarely even ask them?

Non-Sense

The theme is non-sense. It is everywhere once you lock your mind onto it. *A Course in Miracles* says the ego world validates its existence by convincing us that we need its protection from a cruel world. Yet, if you ask the question, "What is inherently fearful about this world *without* the ego and its wars and competitions and separateness?" it will not even answer. Not only will you not receive any answer, but the question will be wiped from your mind. Honestly, why have you not demanded answers to *sensical* questions from your priests, your teachers, your parents, your politicians, yourself? The questions blur together in the ego world; they don't really make sense even though they are sensical. Have you ever asked someone who says they believe in a loving God if they are sometimes afraid of that God? Almost always the response is sure, that's the nature of God. But it's *not* really the nature of God, it's the nature of the ego-created God. The God that the ego has created for us (to keep us safe) is just like the ego, not like a Divine being. The ego God is kind and generous when it wants to be, and ferocious and cruel when it feels justified. And who can predict the changing moods or fickle behavior of the ego-God? It is non-sensical.

Other aspects of our world don't make sense either. For example, consider education? Why do we take little children with their natural sense of wonder and awe and force them to sit up straight, be quiet and only ask questions when they are called upon? And then we can ask only *mandated* questions. The awe and wonder are replaced with compliance and submission. Lifting up the edge of the ego, we see it does not really like those who ask too many questions, who sense divinity in this illusion and who desire to find it. In every country, teachers are among the lowest paid professions. Why is that? They are directly responsible for the next generation of that country's citizens. Shouldn't teaching be a respected and privileged position, where teachers are seriously screened and selected with great care? After all, aren't they pinnacles of highest examples to young minds? And why are students required by law to sit in class, hour after hour, year after year, and then leave school not knowing how to balance a checkbook or read a legal contract, basic knowledge required for living and functioning alone? And why do high schools start so early in the morning and elementary schools start later, when it is teens who cannot get up early and children awake with the dawn? And why are there massive campaigns launched about saving lives by using seatbelts, and most states mandate their use in a moving car, yet school buses do not even come equipped with seat belts? What about those non-senses? Once your mind starts to uncover the motives of the ego-created world, it suddenly becomes ludicrous!

Another example of non-sense is politics. Are all world leaders megalomaniacs? They occupy positions dedicated to guiding and leading *others*, and yet their primary motivation is *self*-promotion. Who set that up? Why is it that the five permanent members of the UN Security Council are the also the world's largest arms suppliers? Why do representatives of the people actually represent the interests of only a few individuals of wealth and power? Who are the people again? And how does it happen that lawmakers make the very laws that they in turn break almost every day? Who would do that in a sensible world?

Why do people work to live? Why do people continue doing work they hate to perpetuate a life simply to support the work they hate? Why do we need medicine to heal a body that supposedly God made? Why are the foods that taste the best considered the worst for our bodies? And vice versa? Why do we buy food that has been sprayed with poison? Why do we teach our children to brush their teeth with toothpaste that contains the second most poisonous element (after only cyanide) known? Do any of these issues make sense? Yes, they exist and we understand them on some level, but how do we understand them at a core level? How do we interpret such inconsistencies of thinking? And why do we accept these inconsistencies as if there were no other options? If we truly are Divine Beings made in the image of the Creator of the Universe, would that Being, capable of only unconditional love, want us to live in chaos and unhappiness? Or is that creator impotent?

That last question is what the ego will ask you. It likes to play the endless loop game. The ego will hand you a question that seems valid and significant—like solving the problems of globalization—only to watch you go around and around with an unsolvable puzzle. You are playing its game then, rather than seeing through it. Lift up the edge of the ego and observe the sleeping dog lying there. You will either see a small and fearful dog, symbolic of the ego's threats and intimidations, or you will see the face of God. Keep looking beyond the ego and its city limits and you will see what it never wants you to know—and that is that you *are* God. And if you knew that, why would you invest anything, anything at all in the ego illusion? If you are God, why do you need a bully to protect you?

However, before you can know you are God, you must create a new concrete reality for yourself and you must get out of the ego town. Like a European city through which I wandered for weeks, the ego town is a myriad of streets and alleys, dead ends and one-way passages winding back upon themselves. As you find your way through a foreign town, identify markers along the way to help you remember your way Home. Identify the ego posts, the pillars of the ego, the edifices to the ego. They will be big and pompous, but that makes them easy to find. Let the mind guide you to locate them, before you know it, you'll have traversed its labyrinth.

"Shall I not have intelligence with the earth? Am I not partly leaves and vegetable mould myself?"

– Henry David Thoreau

5 The Role of Earth and Nature

Most of my life I have read books where Nature, with a capital N, is beloved, all-knowing and sinless because it knows what it is. Each flower, each tree knows what it is and knows that it is here to express itself in glorious flowerness or treeness. I don't disagree with that. I just think most of us defer to Nature in a way that adds more fuel to the self-loathing that humans love to do. Nature is not here to show you up, to make you feel bad because *She* got it and *you* didn't. For example, those precious moments of quiet and solitude that you experience in nature may cause you to feel disgust upon returning to your man-made world. So what is the point, exactly? The point is, you can find lots of reasons to hate yourself no matter what the situation, or how healing it was intended to be.

Let's look at this Earth orb and see where we fit in. Many modern thinkers believe that Earth is simply being tortured by humans until the end of time. It is hard to believe we are not the bad guys when you look at the rate that various species are becoming extinct or the damage being done through deforestation, clear-cutting, mining, pollution, toxic chemicals, to name only a few. But if you step into another way of looking at things, that this is a dreamscape and you are sleep walking, then what is your relationship with Earth? What is the dynamic that produces the healing that allows you to awaken? Could you have created a world that offers an endless variety of possibilities for healing and growth? And could some of those experiences produce more self-loathing and guilt depending upon how you see your lessons and how much you buy into the dream?

Earth is simply a huge learning ground where there is every opportunity for personal or group growth in any incarnation you happen to be experiencing, and at any time. Whatever struggles you may need to assist you along your spiritual journey can be found here. You will find it all here on Earth. And if Earth is the classroom, Nature represents some of our classmates. Let's look at what they offer separately.

When I speak of karma, reincarnation, or various manifestations in a physical body, I am referring to the cycle that occurs inside the Illusion. In Reality, it has no basis, but as we are trying to understand how to step outside the Illusion, knowing what tools and attributes that exist within it will guide us to the willingness to awaken from it. That being said, let's look at the Earth inside our Illusion.

Earth does not need to be fixed. It is not a peaceful planet of quiet inhabitants. It has co-joined the karma of humans to supply the opportunity for optimal growth. Yes, it then holds a similar goal as do humans, and that is spiritual evolution, but while it patiently does its part, it does not resent humans for being here. That is part of its journey. Likewise, we as humans have entwined our journeys with that of the Earth, so as our spiritual evolution progresses and we embody compassion and empathy, we then treat Mother Earth more kindly. We walk this path together.

So what are some of the specific options available here? If forgiveness is the subject you came here to pass, there will be a multitude of possibilities waiting for you wherever you drop your hat. If you have come here to end your dance with violence, there will be more specific families, jobs and experiences for you. If you came here to understand how obsessive the ego can be when you let it have complete control, you may find yourself the head of a powerful country before you realize that you are failing your course.

If you look at the diversity of this globe, you will wrack your mind trying to understand it. How does one understand the differences in economic standing, the differences in ease of physical living around the equator compared to the harshness of living toward the poles, the amount of material abundance in western countries contrasted with the scarcity in third world countries, living in war zones versus pastoral villages of quiet and laziness? Why is materialism not equal for every man? Why is there not peace everywhere? Why are some people persecuted and others worshipped? Why do some people make $30 million a year and yet the people of Madagascar are considered lucky if they make $126 a year? Allow your mind a sabbatical if you are one of those people who try to solve the problems of the world. Those problems are here to provide every experience needed to help you grow individually and collectively. If you looked at it another way, would it change anything? Has anyone ever been able to stop war? Has anyone ever been able to equalize the injustices of man? You could also go to bed every night feeling guilty for eating filet mignon and enjoying it while knowing others in this world suffer intense hunger. Do you really need another reason to hate yourself? Let's stay with the theme that the Earth is a cognizant participant in evolution, spiritual or otherwise.

Let's look at specifics. If you came here to embody faith, true divine faith or trust, as a missing piece in your spiritual growth, would you be plopped down into a sure thing? Would you find yourself in a familial situation where your every need was consistently cared for? Not likely. Instead, let me suggest that you might choose a life where, in order to supply even the most mundane needs, you had to trust someone, you had to put yourself in a place of vulnerability. The experiences might include going from foster home to foster home, lover to lover, or job to job. The insecurities would either overwhelm you and you would shore up for inevitable times of loss or loneliness only to be disappointed again and again, or you would rise to a place of divine faith, knowing that you are guided, loved and directed. The bigger the lesson, the harder the class. Experiences are opportunities for growth, but it doesn't mean you are going to understand them. You don't always succeed as your spirit would prefer. That is part of the reason for this book. If you understood what your lessons were—if you knew that you were being challenged, if you knew there were no victims, but you had a hand in this elaborate game of life—then wouldn't it be easier? Wouldn't knowing these things help you uncover the strengths to try things a different way, the courage to look at experiences with spiritual clarity, the responsibility to own what is happening to you?

Let's say you came here this time to release a repeated theme of betrayal? You have taken the class several times before, but due to societal tendencies (i.e., everyone thinks the same way about betrayal, good vs. bad, etc.) you failed the class according to your own standards. This life finds you repeating it again, probably for the seventh time, which means you have a serious groove in that repeating vinyl record and may find it even harder to look at things differently this time. But what other solution is possible except to be confronted with betrayal again? How else are you going to release that energy? You can talk about it, but talking doesn't change anyone's energy. You can study it; you'll see it happen in others' lives. You can even research it; romance novels are replete with it. But as much as you detest the idea of betrayal, somewhere it must be faced, and at some time it must be seen through the eyes of responsibility and not victimhood. You are co-creating your life, and the Earth willingly participates. Hopefully you will both evolve (sooner than later).

What if you have soldier energy that you have carried for centuries? You define yourself as a soldier, a nationalistic, prideful being who protects and serves his country. But it is not love, so following that route forever is not going to get you Home. Remember, Home or Awakening is only the vibration of love, so to embody war and violence, even if it is in the name of protection or nationalism, it is still not love. So eventually, you will learn about letting the soldier energy go and redefine yourself as something closer to love. Then the Earth must participate. It must say, "You can use my soil, you can slay your bodies on me, you can blow up your bombs on me, but it would be great if your actions would cause some learning." If Earth is a willing participant and not a victim either, then it doesn't judge; it allows and waits. Or perhaps it does not even exist in Reality, but is only part of the dreamscape, the backdrop of the dreamers. But either way, there is cooperative learning and growth going on.

How much violence and war need to occur before the individual or group understands it is only the hamster wheel turning out of control? Maybe an entire war will only afford seven souls the awareness of their lessons. The bombs still blow up, the bodies are still slain, again and again, seven more and then eight. This concept of time, you know, is only man-created. Don't get attached to the idea that after a certain amount of reasonable time, everyone should be evolved. Maybe time does not exist, and it is all happening in one space/moment. Maybe there is only eternity. Maybe the whole thing is a dream, or a nightmare depending on which class you're in, and reality is something altogether different.

Let's look back at Nature for it offers something else. It can also provide learning experiences for you along with its own growth. And Nature holds an element for you different than just the classroom, because these classmates are living, they are life force energy beings like you. So they hold yet another purpose and that is to connect.

Each time you connect with another creature, plant, mineral, element, you are remembering who you are. You share the common thread of life-giving energy and in order to truly connect, you must find this bond. When you sense yourself in these diverse and unusual beings, you feel the divine. So when you connect with nature, if you can let go of the thought, "I am just a lowly humanoid," you promote your divinity. You are sharing a moment of sameness, of caring, of empathy, or of joy and love.

Have you ever met a dog that just takes to you and you to her immediately? You look into those big brown eyes and they seem to hold a massive love for you that you cannot understand with your brain. You feel something well up in you that has no explanation other than simply sharing a moment of love and ecstasy that comes from truly connecting. You try to forget this dog and carry on with your human activities, but you cannot. This dog calls you to be equal for a moment, to find that place where all beings resonate: simple love. For a brief moment you are a dog and she is a human and vice versa. No hierarchy of beings exists, only a connected moment of love. This is what Nature with a capital N can do.

It can also teach you the impermanence of the body. Observing an animal being killed by another animal or simply watching it die of old age can be heart wrenching, especially if you have shared *many* heartfelt moments of love together. But these animals really are saying, "I was never this golden retriever anyway, I was always a spirit connecting with you." And they quietly pass on to a place where their spirit can be free to be in another vehicle, perhaps one grander and more conducive to their spirit.

It always bothers me, no matter how many times I tell myself that it is Nature, when I observe (too late to intervene, as if I even should) a hawk attacking a songbird outside my window. It has happened several times and always shakes me up. It looks so violent, the hawk, with its superior grip, swiftly grabs the little unsuspecting sparrow and starts ripping its head off with its beak. Because, as you can probably tell, I prefer little innocent songbirds. What amazes me every time is that while the sparrow is not yet dead, it does not struggle or scream. Quietly, it just vacates its vehicle. Likewise, the other sparrows do not go into a screeching song, they scatter of course, but within moments of the hawk's disappearance, they come back into sight and commence eating again. Once my husband and I were up in the mountains and we were talking about this idea of what happens to the spirit prey is absorbed into the predator, and the larger predator is then connected spiritually with the prey. *Just* at that moment an eagle flew directly in front of us, snatched up a mouse and flew off with it. "Well," I said, "there you have it, the eagle and the mouse now share consciousness."

So what about us? As we supposedly occupy the top of the food chain, how do we connect without devouring our energy being? Well, you actually could connect while devouring, if it is done with conscious thought and honor, thanking the animal that has given its body for your nourishment. Think for a moment about your leather shoes or your cowhide couch. Was there some being that you could be grateful for and even appreciate every time you put on your shoes or stretch out on the couch? Your mindfulness will make it blessed and will bring the connection.

Other connections are possible as well. Every time you relate with some part of Nature, whether you are staring at a river or letting a ladybug crawl on your hand, you are being offered the opportunity to connect, to let the lesson of love be admitted. The key is to forget your maturity for a moment. Have you ever gotten on the floor and played with a child, eye to eye? This act sets aside your adulthood for a time. Take one more step. It really shouldn't be that difficult because some of us share qualities with some animals. Have you ever known someone who is slinky like a cat or loyal like a dog? They might be cool, aloof and catlike or eager and completely open like a dog? Consider your cat while it is sitting near you, watching you or laying in your lap. Take a moment to contemplate being a cat; what qualities do you have that are like a cat? Maybe you are shy or like to be alone, or you like to be in control, or you enjoy being stroked (in your own time), or you love to investigate things with cat-like curiosity. Even dog people may discover that they possess qualities like a cat. So now you share not only the life-giving energy of the universe with a cat, but you also share common traits.

Now imagine the cat looking at you and wondering what traits it may have with this human sitting there on the couch? Does it enjoy eating? Does it like to daydream? Does it like your best friend as much as you do? Does it like to lounge on Sunday mornings in the sun coming through the kitchen window? What is the thread your cat will find with you?

Once while walking my neighbor's dog, I was pondering some thoughts about people's Higher Selves. Lost in thought, I looked down at this little Shih Tzu, who does not think of himself as a dog at all. He was appropriately named Hercules. All of us in the neighborhood call him a little man, because to call him a dog might cause him psychological damage. He has a distinct personality and I wondered about his Higher Self. Many times I have spoken to it, to let him know when his family will be home so he won't mope while I am watching him. I've even alerted him of changes, but I have never actually taken the time to *visualize* his Higher Self. So on this particular day, I was walking past a fire hydrant with him and I wondered what Hercules' Higher Self was like. At that moment, there appeared a full-length, 6-foot tall being of light walking right beside me! It was *not* on the collar at the end of the leash. It was not a dog-spirit looking thing, but an upright being of dignity and honor right beside me. I have to say, after knowing this dog, I was not surprised, but I will certainly never think of dogs the same way again. They are not our inferiors, they are alive and embody the life-force energy of the Divine just like you and me. They have just chosen vehicles with limited speech, that's all.

Every time you take a moment out of your busy life to connect, whether it is with your own children or a neighbor's dog, you are reinforcing the life energy of us all. You are connecting to the thread that makes us divine and you are finding the equality in us all. I remember looking deep into the eyes of an infant of a patient of my husband. I went in deep and began to feel the whole life and the history and wisdom of this little child. He awed me with an ancient spirit. My mind then went to the circumstances of his present birth, not that he wasn't loved, but he had entered a difficult economic and austere physical environment. I started to feel a sadness for him, and he began to cry. Then I realized that he was picking up on my thoughts, so I snapped out of my pity for him and began to consciously dwell on his mother's love for him, so genuine and real. In my mind, I told him that no matter what the circumstances of his physical life, he had an incredible opportunity to connect with the love of the Divine, especially after having experienced a love like his mother's. Whew, I extricated myself from that one! He must have understood me, because he stopped crying.

Have you ever caught a mouse or has a bird gotten trapped in your chimney? Have you ever watched a spider from inside your window? Have you looked for her again each day? Have you watched a tree grow from a sprig? Have you been party to its first bud? Have you ever transplanted something that would have been plowed under otherwise? Have you ever seen a tarantula or a rattle snake in Nature? Have you studied them, watched the way they move, felt less afraid once you saw them in their world? Have you ever watched a hummingbird build a nest and then wait with anticipation for its babies? Have you ever sat and stared at a bug, or watched the trail of an ant? What about rocks, do you feel peaceful when sitting in a rocky area with large slabs of ancient minerals surrounding you?

Have you ever connected with a Bristlecone Pine tree? They are some of the oldest trees on the planet, and some are believed to be older than 4000 years old. To connect with a Bristlecone, you have to slow your energy down a lot; you need to sit and quiet your inner self because they are such slow growers and your active vibration is too fast for them. Sit near one for 15 minutes and wait for a connection; it is finally like a very slow pulse you are barely aware of. But to do so means your life will never be the same again. You have been touched by the pulse of a Bristlecone Pine tree.

Connecting with *any* living thing will bring richness to your life, and it will also nourish your spirit. The idea is to grow the soul power; connecting and allowing are ways to succeed. Next time you are standing in the checkout line at the grocery store and a 3-month old baby espies you and stares you down, don't turn away. Let yourself be scrutinized, tuned into, and connected with. You may have known each other well in another life, who knows? It could be a spirit identity check!

As you connect with life all around you, allow yourself to feel its bigness without making reference to your own smallness. Don't look at the sun and in that instant make the comparison of how small you are in relation to the impressively gigantic, all-powerful sun. If you really are connected with the sun, you will find that you have as powerful a radiant light in *you* as does the sun. In fact, if you really let it out, the sun would have to squint in your presence. In other words, if you knew the divine lightness and radiant godness that you are, you would see that you are brighter and more everlasting than the sun. Yes, the giant star that lights our solar system! You are brighter than that! You would mirror back more light than the moon, you would be stronger than the trees, and you'd have more courage than the bears. But until you know this, you can settle for being the same as: for being courageous as a bear, for being as quiet as a fox, and as wise as a beaver, for being as devoted as a pair of swans, as romantic as two ravens, as curious as a chipmunk and as delightful as a marmot!

Nature is here for many reasons, and to create an opportunity to connect without self-loathing or deference is as divine a reason as any. Earth herself is here, and learning your lessons not only elevates you along your journey, but also evolves the very planet that assists. So don't miss the lesson for the size of its body. Taking 32 seconds to stoop and connect, to move a caterpillar out of harm's way even, makes the experience of living in Earth School not only much richer, but it makes the lessons much easier.

"It is essential to remember that only the mind can create...the soul is already perfect, and therefore does not require correction. The body does not really exist except as a learning device for the mind."

— A Course in Miracles

6 The Role of the Body

Comforting as it may seem, the body has been placed in an elevated position in the physical world. We all have bodies, some dysfunctional and laden with health difficulties, others healthy and robust. But is it *who* you are? Are you the composite of your physique, facial structure, muscle tone, fat count, the length of your legs relative to the torso? Or are you more than that? Who are you really? As you have been discovering, the essence of you is only *spirit*. The body is simply a vehicle. It is no more important along your journey than the comfortable mid-sized car sitting inside your garage. Several reasons lead me to dash these dreams of your body and its diets and workouts as being you.

First, a day will come when you choose to leave this cycle of birth and death, as Buddha called it. You will want to return to who you truly are, and you'll desire it above all else, but you won't have the foggiest idea how to get there. An important step along that journey is to realize that you are not your body. In doing so, you will reapportion power to your spirit as you come to understand *the spirit* is who you are. Secondly, the body can actually *help* you along your journey. Just as the car can transport you in relative comfort and quiet to your chosen destination, so can your physical body.

Perhaps it is not fair to start this section by declaring that you are not your body. Some people have spent many dollars and many more hours turning that physical mass they were born with into a sculpted, beautiful object of adoration. You might be saying, "What about that? How do I get my money back?" This discussion isn't meant to degrade the body in any way; it is a vehicle. If you were transporting a holy personage, and you were the assigned driver, you would be very cautious and you would take care of the vehicle you were using to make sure it transported you safely. But would you risk your life or someone you loved for your car? Would you allow your arm to be cut off to save your car from a crash? Let's put things into perspective.

If you can understand that you are not your body, you have actually freed yourself. Just the thought that you are a spirit brings a sense of freedom to your mind, knowing that a body cannot contain you or imprison you, as many bodies feel that they are doing. The important thing to remember is that who you are is a spirit having a human experience, not a body occasionally having a spiritual experience, which it often feels like.

I bring this up because this premise is elemental in your journey Home. You may have had hundreds, perhaps thousands, of lives where you have played the endless loop tape again and again. To get new footage you have to change something. One of the primary changes needed to turn off the repeat cycle is to realize you are not a body. This means, first of all, that you are giving more credence to your spirit than your body, that you are giving it more power. When you give something more power, it can grow. When something grows, it contains more space. When something contains more space, you and everyone who sees it cannot deny it. Thusly you become filled with that and nothing else. You begin to embrace the essence of the spirit more each hour, each day until the majority of your experiences are spirit-led. That means your vibration, or what you resonate with, is higher, less dense like the body, and higher in frequency like the spirit. Do you see how to get Home now? You eliminate everything that is not Home and all that's left is the essence of Home. Let me reinforce here that Home is not a place outside yourself, it is simply *correct perception*.

All the rules for all your lives have said the same thing: you are a body, deal with it. But now I am saying, you are *not* your body and don't buy into anything that says it is. You are not your body, bodies are vehicles, and most people buy into the idea that when you select a particular model you are stuck with it. No matter how you think you can alter it, it keeps morphing back to the original body type. What about people who do change their bodies, like Charles Atlas, the skinny kid getting sand kicked in his face? He became a sculpted muscle man leading the way for other underdogs everywhere. It's just like those stretch limos, the ones as long as three vehicles with a hot tub and bar inside. Like Charles, they believe that the vehicle is made for modification. But before you believe that, you have to have power over your vehicle. And before you can have power over your vehicle, you have to have some degree of knowing that *you*, the essential you, are *not* your vehicle. Charles Atlas must have known that deep inside that puny kid was the heart of a large man. His body did not reflect it, but his knowing did.

Here is more impetus to accept that you are not your body. If you believe you are not your body, you can modify it. You can imagine another model and it will become another model, whether it's one without cancer or 40 pounds lighter, it's your choice. It is not who you are anyway; the essential you does not change. If you have allocated more power to your spiritual self and less to your body, then when you accept the belief that you no longer need to get sick, who obeys? The more powerful one obeys. And if that is your body, then your body decides; if your spirit is more powerful, meaning it owns the most amount of energy, then you no longer get sick. Children and animals are not exempt. They are a compilation of beliefs and misperceptions that have brought them into the vehicles they presently occupy.

What if you have a body that you abhor? You associate yourself with that body, but it is no more your body than a car you inherited that you have always despised. There may be a reason you are driving it, just as there most likely is a reason you are living in this body, but it doesn't mean you have to degrade yourself to the lowness of the vehicle. And here's an added benefit. When you live more, knowing that you are not a body, you give more credence to the spirit. As you give more credence to this divine part of you, your spirit, you also give more credence to it in others. And the more you believe this spirit exists and is powerful, the more you can actually *see* it. What begins to form is an overlay of the spirit upon the place where the body was. So what I am saying is, bodies you come into contact with begin to look more divine and more lovely, including, but not limited to, your own.

The Body as an Alarm Clock

You may ask me, "Okay, Julie, now what do I do? I believe you and something feels familiar about this old thought. How do I allocate power to my spirit?" If you really want to embark upon the part of the journey that allows the spirit to soar, to take you Home, to fill you with love and peace beyond your deepest imagining, freeing you from the chains of the body, then you are ready. This is the point where the alarm clock comes in. Every time you think of the body in any way, allow it to be an alarm clock that says, "Beep-beep-beep—reallocate energy—beep-beep-beep." When you think about your stomach and how it feels distended from food or bloating, when you think about flossing your teeth, when you think about needing to brush your hair or shave your legs, your alarm clock goes off. Now you just have to set it, and it is quite easy. You simply state that you want to hear an alarm message every time you think of your body. It will happen. In fact, you may be alarmed yourself to learn how often the average person thinks of their body or bodily desires. It is almost constantly. And what if you could take all that thought energy and turn it over to your spirit self? Can you imagine how different life would be?

Let's get more specific. Let the beeper go off in your mind when you think you are hungry, when you begin to feed the body's mouth, when you feel sleepy, when you berate yourself for eating too much, when you judge whether or not something is healthy for your body. Remember, the body is simply a vehicle, a vessel for your soul. Joy and love are elements of the soul, and if something brings you joy, then by all means do it more often, without guilt, please. Do you have to eat salads because they provide the necessary roughage for a healthy bowel system even if you can't stand lettuce another day? Remember the body is only a vehicle. It does not determine *anything*. Your car cannot drive itself (although some day it may do so) without you at the wheel providing the necessary guidance. That is the same as your body getting instructions from the spirit. When you are sick or overweight, don't blame the body, the body is only following directions. It has no mind of its own, and I am not referring to the organ known as the brain. The body is just a vehicle. And even though it is wise as a car owner to maintain your vehicle, change the oil every so many miles, check the tire pressure, clean it, and fill it with fuel, you don't need to wake up in the night and go check on it in the garage to see if it needs anything.

Let's go back to the alarm clock and an exercise that, in the beginning, will be overwhelming to do. Every other minute you are going to be interrupted with a body beep. What you do when you hear this beep is to chose a mantra, or a saying that reminds you that your spirit would like some attention. You can say something like, "I am not a body," or, "I am a spirit," or, "I am a spirit having a human experience," or any number of things that remind you of your divine spirit nature. "I am connected to the Divine and the Divine is connected to me." And then you repeat that mantra and give the same amount of time and thought to the recognition of the spirit. It is like saying "Oh, I see you there and remember how fortunate I am to have you, thank you." Then you go about your life, probably for about 32 seconds until you hear another body beep. Do the same thing, say, "thanks," and reallocate thoughts to your spirit. "Oh yeah, I *am* a spirit, I forgot." Later, after forgetting to pay attention to the body beeps all day, you push back from the table after dinner, thinking, "Man, I really ate too much." Beep-beep-beep. Remind yourself here that spirits are light, that they are non-physical and cannot feel stuffed; remind yourself that you are only experiencing this feeling, but it is not *who you are*. Do you see the difference? If you think you are a stuffed blimp, you will easily go into self-loathing. If you know you are a spirit watching this bizarre movie, then you should have less propensity to hate yourself over it. I have found that the immediate pain goes away, you start to feel lighter, and the stuffed feeling doesn't take hold.

Also, it works well with acute pains like wasp stings or stubbed toes. "I am *not* my body, I am a spirit, I am *not* my body, I am a spirit," and the pain seems to have less power. Some say that eventually you get to the point where you could actually feel no pain at all.

The point is, the body is a servant, a vessel, and it is here to serve you along your soulful journey. Somewhere in this crazy mixed up world, the rules all got changed and the directions got lost and we became slaves to our bodies. And instead of caring for our bodies as we would a devoted servant and friend, we loathe the power it has over us. We treat it not so nicely, we punish it and cater to it, we give in and let it blackmail us. Who knows where all this began, but take a look at this vehicle you have chosen. Do you like it? If you were in the lot picking out a vehicle, would you pick yours? What do you want to do with it? Isn't that what car salesmen always ask you, "What are you planning to use this car for?" If you are going to go long distances, you'll want a cruising car, quiet with good gas mileage, comfortable seats. If you are in the testosterone high of your life, you will want something that is loud and draws attention to you, comfort is not important, but brightness is. If you are in a service industry, you will need something capable of transporting your products in the most efficient manner. Do you have lots of kids, or love to take your neighbors' kids to school along with yours? You might need a mini van or other utility vehicle, and so on. Now look at your body this way. What do you use it for? If you are doing table dances in Vegas, it definitely will need to be outfitted a tad differently than if you are hauling slabs of concrete all day.

So, if you are happy with your body vehicle, take good care of it, but remember, you are boss. If you are not happy with it, know the more you allocate power to your spirit, the more you will be capable of modifying your body. And if you are somewhere in between, let your body assist you by beeping at you and allowing you to take over when you should be in control. At any stage of the body game, let your body be your alarm clock to remind you that you are obsessing with your car again. Remind yourself that the destination is more important than the wheels you use to get there. Where are you going anyway? Do you want your history to repeat itself for another thousand years or so? If so, then let your body take you there, it is all it knows. But your spirit will take you to ultimate freedom.

Body in Pain and Sickness

Frequently people actually commit to a journey of a spiritual nature because they feel forced to do so. They feel left with no other choice. The body threatens with extreme pain or disease and it becomes a wakeup call that whatever format life has taken before, it can no longer continue. Many people have admitted that this end-of-the-rope condition forced a severe life change. This is when you feel the body has failed you, and it can no longer support the wishes and will of the spirit that inhabits it.

The physical body has no power or will of its own. It only responds to the messages it is sent. The body does not raise you from your bed in the morning. It is your mind that says, "I need to get up now or I will be late, or I will be groggy if I stay here any longer." And the muscles obey the will of the mind. When you need to run for a bus because you know if you miss it you will have to walk home or wait 2 hours for the next one, your legs engage in top priority speed driven by the will of the mind, not by the body. The body doesn't care if you wait by the bus stop 2 hours or if you wait by the bar or kitchen table. The body has no will.

So now, when you fall ill, or become overwhelmed with a life threatening disease, what has happened? Why can't medical doctors explain why *you* got cancer? Was it genetics, diet, health, stress? No common thread has been identified; cancer is one of those looming darknesses that just seems to descend upon you when you least expect it, or that's what it feels like anyway. When a body ceases to be healthy, it is simply reflecting an unhealed mind. The natural state of a healed mind is health. Since the purpose of a body is a vehicle or tool, and we create our own world, why would we create illness and pain? The mind is part ego images and beliefs and part mental and karmic beliefs. To look to the body for answers is truly like looking to the battleground for the soldiers long gone. Go ahead and search the battleground, but you won't find any answers. You need to look deeper. What does the mind hold that allows the body to become diseased?

The mind holds beliefs that allow for pain, sorrow and death. When your body is even a teeny bit ill, it is a message to access the mind, not punish the body. Thank the body for the early warning message. The alternative is the much later warning message of cancer or heart attack.

Elements Involved in Creation

Let's look at the elements in creating misperceptions in the mind. The first element is the *body*. It is a neutral playing ground as we have discussed, a clean slate, for playing out the beliefs you hold. It repairs or maintains health according to your unconscious beliefs. The body has no will, it simply responds. If you hold an internal image of yourself that you are ugly or fat, your body will accommodate you. If you hold an image of yourself that you are weak, your body will oblige. Mostly, we are held hostage by the unconscious belief of who we think we are. Images of self-identity, or rather, misperceptions of identity are always the culprit of an unhealed mind. To even entertain an image of yourself that is weak or inadequate in any way is to not have a clear image of the truth of who you are. But that is the goal of this book, to guide you down a path of understanding where you can meet your true self at the end.

The second element involved in creation is the *spirit*. The spirit is the Essence of you, the formless self, the connection to your Source. It is the Self that needs no healing. It is You as you were created originally. You feel it in the form of nudges, intuition, guidance, and heart-felt desire. It is compelled by a higher calling, from your own self as well as from guidance from your metaphysical helpers and teachers. Its purpose is always the same, to bring your awareness back to the divine self it truly is, to reunite with all of creation energy. It can use the body as a vehicle to help this process.

Enter a third element, the *ego*. The presence of the ego is why the body has become a battlefield. The conflict between the purpose of the spirit and that of the ego creates confusion and attack. The ego has its own desires. Having desires is actually what it does the best. In fact, it wants to just have desires, but not to fulfill them. As long as there is no fulfillment, there will still be the need to keep desiring. The ego has material desires, it wants personality recognition, as well as attention and accolades. Everything it wants is temporary and fleeting so that the need to keep desiring continues so it can have control and power. So these desires of the spirit to return to some ambiguous, united, peaceful and fulfilled place are *not* congruent with the desires of the ego. Who pays the price for this conflict? The body. And who is the only one you can see and blame and make feel guilty? The body.

So when the body is not well, it is a call to look inward, into an old belief that is actively controlling your manifest experience. We will talk more about challenging old controlling beliefs, but first simply accept the awareness that the body does not hold the key to your greater healing. It may be an early warning signal, or an alarm clock, but it only responds to how it has been programmed.

SECTION TWO
TRANSFORMING
PERCEPTIONS

"It is you who must make the effort. The masters only point the way."

– Buddha

7 Maturing the Ego

The maturity of the ego is a necessary part of awakening. To understand the power and control the ego has over you, you have to become familiar with how it controls you and take back some authority until eventually all the decision making power is in the capable hands of the spirit. Warring or attacking the ego only engages it even further. Allowing it to control your thoughts, actions, responses and desires simply keeps you in an endless game. To step out of the repeating pattern and leave behind the tiresome dissatisfaction the ego affords gives you control of your life and you begin to Awaken.

Bringing the ego to maturity makes all your lessons easier to learn and makes the whole journey far less painful. If you assume that you balk at your lessons because they are hard, painful or unpleasant, maturing the ego makes the experiences more palatable, thus ensuring that you will pass your tests easily and be ready for the next assignment. First, let's examine clues to recognize an immature ego acting out. Then we'll look at ways to proceed that will not only bring discipline and maturity, but will also expedite the whole awakening process. You may associate with some of these egoic propensities more than others.

Defensiveness

One of the first clues to recognize an ego refusing to learn its lesson is the quality of its response. And you may not be aware that you are being defensive until you understand all that it encompasses. Your ego is being defensive when someone makes a suggestion to you or brings up an idea different than yours and you respond with excuses: excuses why you never tried that, or why you decided upon the course of action you took, or why their idea won't work. Any kind of excuse constitutes defensiveness even if you feel it is noble or worthy. That behavior is defensiveness; it is defending your way.

This aspect is easier to see in someone else, so let's look at a third party. You are having a conversation with a friend and she brings up her long distance phone carrier with chagrin; she is unhappy and complaining about the service she receives. You have had this same experience so you share with her your story and how you eventually changed to a new carrier and how much happier you have been. You expect an applaud, "Great, you've already done this, you've saved me the trouble, now I can learn from you." But what you actually hear is a string of reasons why your solutions wouldn't work for her, particularly in her specific situation at this particular time. Her reasons really don't seem justified to you, but keep her firmly in the grasp of this unpleasant situation. There you have it, a perfect case of defensiveness. And once you identify it as an ego/personality trait, you may realize you do it as often as breathing.

Here's another example. You are having lunch with your mother. She makes a kind suggestion that you should tell your father some detail of your personal life that you have been avoiding. Inside you know she is right, but before you can even acknowledge her comment, your ego is off and running. "Mom, first of all, it's none of your business. Secondly, you don't know how mad dad will be when he hears it and his health isn't very good, and he doesn't need to worry about my situation with everything he has going on at work right now, and besides, it may resolve itself"…and on and on. She only made a suggestion. It was a personal observation that you could either accept or not. To defend your position is to set up a sense of righteousness on your part. Your mother did not mean to attack. She was truly only trying to smooth a difficult relationship by bringing honesty into it.

I'll present one more example before we look at what to do with our defensive and somewhat immature ego. You are at work, and you notice that the copier was left without paper. You suggest to a co-worker who works closest to it that he could keep an eye out for refilling the paper. It is just an efficient suggestion for smoother running of the organization. He replies quite pitifully that he was sorry and wasn't paying attention. he explained that he had gone to the men's room just then and had been thinking about his bills, and he would do his best to keep a better look out, etc. His response isn't attacking, but it is still defensive. He is defending a position, the one that says he is trying to be an efficient worker, but was caught off guard for one minute. Maybe no one ever suggested that because he was the closest to the machine he was best suited for the job, or maybe you didn't mean to imply that he wasn't doing an excellent job; but his ego did not want to be perceived as a slaggart. It wanted you to know it too. Defensiveness.

Although I will illustrate with more examples as we proceed, truly, it is so natural that, until it gets drilled into your mind, it has become an unconscious process. How do you mature this out-of-control beast who only wants to be seen as the best, most thoughtful and kindest, or the toughest and most self-sufficient? You formulate another response. First, you must recognize that you have been defending your position, making excuses or generally arguing with the suggestion or comment. Look at it from the other person's perspective, and there is always another person. What was that person trying to say and why? Were they making an honest suggestion? Do they care what your excuse is? Does the way you have been doing it before have any bearing? Do you really care what is being suggested? Sometimes people are in a habit of finding the most optimum way of doing every little thing and they constantly recommend their way as a way of life (we will discuss this egoic trait later). When confronted, you can simply make note by saying, "Thank you, that's noted." It isn't necessary to illuminate your thought process by explaining why you do what you do; they really don't care and that's not what they're about. Defending only allows room for attacking, and ultimately, we are looking for joy, peace of mind and happiness. Attacking does not co-exist with these other attributes.

Most of the time, people are trying to be helpful. They want to connect and help others learn from their mistakes, and making suggestions is one way to do that. When someone offers you advice or suggestions, instead of starting your response with, "But…," stop and ask the ego to step back for a moment. Then graciously acknowledge that you heard the comment and appreciate it. If the advice is something you might want to consider, say, "I will certainly consider that." If it is one you would never entertain, say, "Thank you, I appreciate your concern," or something along those lines. Remember, the key is to be aware that it is happening and choose a response other than defensiveness. Defending a position is **never** required. Who would you ever need to explain yourself to? Whose business is it really?

Let's say someone gives you some suggestion that stings. It stings because it may have some truth to it. You don't like the way they presented it, but there is something there to consider. You now must deal with the ego's sting, or woundedness before you can honestly look at what they are suggesting. This step is important: a wounded ego will want to strike back! We'll explore how we handle criticism later, but what about this defensiveness? Perhaps it's manifested in spears and swords. At this point, it is best to end the conversation until you can compose yourself; your misbehaving ego needs a time-out. Picture your immature ego as a child. You may have to remove this child, your ego self (along with your other body parts) into another room.

Defensiveness is an automatic response. It starts with, "But...I only...that's because...I know, but...the reason I didn't was because..." When you catch yourself responding that way, stop and say simply, "Thank you, I'll take that into consideration." It will also stop the never-ending cycle of the 'my way versus their way' conversation that inevitably ensues. Keep in mind the forgiveness concept. Even if you get half way into a whole defensive strategy, wake up, let go and bring the maturity discipline to the ego; then silently forgive yourself for being defensive. This process instantly sets up a dynamic of gentleness. Forgiving yourself brings the element of softness towards you and then to the one with whom you are speaking, even if no one ever knows what is going on. It does not allow the atmosphere of defensiveness (which is a form of attack, because it recognizes the other person as an offender) to remain.

The idea here is to bring awareness to the self so that you can understand and learn your lessons. With the ego always acting up and interfering with the process, you often avoid or delay your messages because you have harpooned the messenger. Listen. Allow for the message to be heard, then determine if it has merit for you personally or not. Allow the messenger to go free, unharmed.

Criticism

How well do you handle criticism? That's a huge issue for some, but not a problem for others. Some people may not handle any form of criticism or constructive suggestions. Others have hot spots, and still others don't seem to hear or care about criticism at all. Let's look at criticism as a learning tool. It is important because the input of others can assist or correct you before you get too engrained or even lost in a negative behavior trait. We all know this logically, but once you involve an immature ego, criticism takes on a very different form: it looks like an attack. And when we are attacked we prepare to retaliate. Perhaps a trigger effect is going on behind the scenes. When someone offers criticism, the emotional body is alerted to become involved and the ego passes the ball to the feeler. There are many different responses to criticism. These are just some I have noted, observing myself and by listening to my clients and watching the energy as they relate a story where they were criticized.

Everyone at some time has been criticized, justly or not. Let's start with an example. You are working for a boss who likes things done a particular way. Frequently, she is curt about her suggestions and does not feel the need for explanation, so the suggestions sometimes seem cruel and insensitive. She suggests that you stop doing a certain activity on Monday mornings because it involves more time away from your desk. Instead she wants it done on Friday when your absence would be less of a problem. You feel like this request came out of left field. You are conscientious, you have always done a good job and feel you are being taken as a loafer, or someone who is careless about decisions. You want to justify (defend) your position, but instead, you are left alone with your emotions since your boss has already left the room. Your victim image says, "What did *I* do?" You're left wondering what to do. Do you cry? Do you get angry? Do you want to destroy something of hers? If you heard her saying this same thing to someone else, it would seem logical and of no consequence. But when it is aimed at you, it feels like a direct attack at your job skills and your *ego*. Remember the ego is that part of you that projects you as being bigger, better, smarter, more good looking: comparing, contrasting and judging. You don't want someone judging *you*.

To allow the ego to be in charge during times of constructive criticism or *suggestion*, as I prefer to call it, is to lose the lesson altogether. You have heard the speaker speak, but did not register what was said. Do you want to hear it later, louder? That's what will have to happen. Then your self-indulgent ego will really be upset. Perhaps a message is lurking here. It may not be about rearranging your schedule at all, it may be about learning the lesson of humility, or being ready for some synchronous event that you would have missed had you not been available on Monday. Who knows? Lessons are as personal as the individual, yet they all lead to the same place, our highest selves.

Often correction or criticism has a positive intent. Occasionally, the person offering the suggestion is way off base, but let's stick with criticism that has a positive potential. Everything has a positive potential, depending upon what you make of it. What I mean to say is, let's not dwell on those who think they are innocent. It has no bearing on the lesson. Let's say that someone you care about or respect feels comfortable enough with you to say what's on their mind. They tell you that you dominate the conversation, not only with them, but with other people in the conversation. They tell you that even though they do indeed love you, they want to give their opinion some airtime, and they feel that others want the same courtesy.

When you hear about someone else, you barely miss a beat, "Oh really? Then what did she say?" But when it is directed to you, or your ego rather, it feels offensive, uncalled for and downright mean. Your response may be varied. You could get upset right back and start listing every negative trait this person has ever exhibited since third grade, you could become silent and pouty, or you could get angry. All of these reactions are of the ego self. They are not bad or good, but if we are going to try to mature the ego, then something else needs to happen here.

As with being defensive, you know that your ego self has become alarmed and is in protection mode. If you cannot talk it down, then you have to sit it out. If nothing about this other person's comment registers as befitting you or it's nothing you care to do anything about, then simply disregard it, change the subject, or thank the other person for their honesty. If the comment *does* register as a personality trait that infuriates you, or that you are aware of but can't seem to control, then it may hurt more. Rationalizing to the speaker is not really the solution. Nothing you come up with will make this person take back what they said, unless it is just to get you to stop reacting as you are. Being defensive is not a solution. Being vulnerable and saying, "Yeah, I know I do that, what do you suggest?" probably isn't going to work either. The ego does not become vulnerable when it perceives itself as being attacked. So what are the options?

Bookmark the comment, discipline your emotional response, if possible, and analyze why this comment, criticism, suggestion, or whatever you call it, has hurt you so much. Then when no one is around, you can expose your vulnerable spot. Accusing the other person as being just jealous because you are more interesting is *not* an option. If your mind is fixated on the other person, your ego still needs maturing. Let it finish it's mental tirade and then be honest about why you are feeling wounded. What you can or cannot do about it is really a question of where you are on your journey, how capable you believe you are of really changing a personality trait, and many other things. The key to the maturation process is taking responsibility for the hurt feeling. No one *made* you feel hurt. It is not someone else's fault that you don't like them anymore. It is the ego trying to create separation wherever it can. The soul-self wants to grow and unite, the ego wants to blame and isolate. Keep these truths in mind when you feel yourself growing distant. Is it your soul doing that, or more likely, is it your ego; punishing, judging, comparing?

Let's take another example, but watch it from the sidelines. Your neighbors walk out of their house just as they see a pedestrian walking a dog. The dog has just used their front lawn as an outhouse and the neighbor suggests to the dog's owner that he might come back and remove what his dog has left behind. As an innocent bystander, you think that your neighbor has every right to make this direct suggestion, however confrontational it may seem. Your neighbor even smiled a thank you in advance. As the incident unravels, two other pedestrians come waltzing around the corner and clearly see what is transpiring. The neighbor doesn't want to lose any ground to the dog's owner. And you, the next-door neighbor, are outside gardening, so now there is an audience. The dog owner's ego feels outnumbered. Even if it *is* the right thing to do scooping up Lassie's remains, too many people are now watching and make it feel like a serious loss to the ego. The immature ego will yell back and keep walking away, refusing to capitulate to peer pressure. Then Mr. Dog-Owner will seethe all the way home, convince himself what a nag this old so-and-so neighbor is, and remind himself to avoid that street for a good long time. In contrast, consider what his mature ego would do, or even his ego in Maturity School? He would take a gulp (that's swallowing pride) and return, baggie in hand and apologize. He may turn the conversation to the lovely yard and flowers of your neighbors. Or if he doesn't have a bag, he could wave a hand of acknowledgment and promise to return with a baggie and remove the offense. The harm is only done to an imaginary ego. Your neighbor only wants to connect in a healthy and honest way, and not feel taken advantage of. The ego only wants to separate, leaving the doggie remains and pride in tact. We must acknowledge this formula for childish egoic behavior and find an alternative.

What if you receive a suggestion that is something you don't want to do? You have every right not to do it, but your response is what we are working on. Let's look at another example. Let's say you are a very emotional person. This fact is not good or bad, it's just an assessment of how you usually respond to things. When you are criticized, your first response may be to cry. You want to be perfect; you really want to be good; why can't you do everything exactly as it is expected of you? When someone offers criticism, all these thoughts run their endless-loop video in your head. The only thing perfect about this imperfect world is that every lesson we could possibly need is perfectly orchestrated for us, by us. And that's the only way this world is perfect. Everything is exactly as it should be, but it is not utopia. Why should you behave perfectly? Is it even something worth striving for? And what is perfect? Who is the standard? So when your response to a suggestion is emotional turbulence, two things will happen. One, the person who made the suggestion will not likely offer a suggestion again, and two, you will miss your lesson because you are busy blowing your nose. The emotional component often is a way to get the ego off the hook and turn the light on the emotional self. It also makes the offender feel sorry for you, lessening the impact of the criticism on your ego. Pretty soon, you don't remember being corrected at all.

What do you do as a maturing ego? You can bring the correction into the classroom, and take it out of the emotionally indulgent place of imperfection that it seeks automatically. You ask your emotional self to refrain, there really is nothing to feel sad or sorry about. If you feel compelled, this is a good place to add the forgiveness thought. Forgive yourself for not feeling perfect. You are *divine*, remember? What is perfection if not that? Silently forgive the other person for feeling compelled to correct you and thank them for assisting you along your journey. The ego has now been matured at the Maturity School rather than being indulged and avoided. Once again, the key is not to blame anyone, including yourself. There doesn't have to be a victim and an assailant. Can't there be souls guiding and assisting each other along the journey home? So in looking at your ego in relation to criticism, it is important to be honest about how you respond, not what you do about it. Right now, we are just maturing your ego. Once you can respond in a mature, more soulful approach, the rest follows a lot easier.

How do you Begin your Sentences?

That's a funny question and it is not a trick. Start paying attention to how often you begin a sentence with the word "I" or "My." In fact, try to write a letter to someone without starting a sentence with "I". The process becomes really creative and forces you to ask about them. Also, notice how often your conversations include "me" and "mine." This little awareness is an excellent exercise to assist maturing the ego and it isn't really that painful. It is a creative way to change your communication process. You will notice it in others too, and it will remind you how often the ego is present in our communications. Remember it is natural for the ego to isolate, segregate and compare. So if you are conscious of a different way of communicating, you allow the soul to be more active and that brings the energy of connecting, touching and learning that you are the same, not different.

This exercise will assist the creativity of your conversations, because instead of recounting what you did, what you ate, where you went and at what time you did something, it allows for conversations of another nature. It allows *feeling* questions to be asked, which permits your partner in conversation to respond energetically by guiding the conversation to a more meaningful place instead of recounting shallow and senseless calendar events. Food is a connection for my family, and if it connects, then it is not feeding the ego; it is reminding us of our commonalities. But if you let the conversation revolve around all *your* meals since last Tuesday, you become ego-centered. Find creative ways to connect, be aware of your ego habits and do not chastise yourself. Simply adjust when possible and remember when you can.

Offering Advice

Some people enjoy determining the most optimum way of doing something and offering that method to others, whether or not they ask. Some people genuinely like to be helpful and see it as part of their job. Others truly feel that they know the *right* way to do everything. Still others may just be looking for a helpful way to connect that makes them feel important and needed at the same time. Whatever their reason your next step in our Ego Maturity School is to consider the giver's motivation, method and frequency of their advice.

It will be up to you to determine which is correct for you. We can only make assumptions about other people and their motivation. Let's consider the motivation that may promote a lot of advice giving: the belief that your way is best. The ego must be present because comparison and judging are involved. One way is best, another way must be *less* best. How do you know if you just want to be helpful or if you have a vested interest in seeing something performed the most optimum way? If someone implements your suggestion, do you become fonder of this person? Do you feel they are smarter, wiser than others to follow your guidance? Do you secretly feel slighted if they select another method of doing something other than the one you outlined? Ask yourself these questions along with the real core issue: do you believe your way is often the best way?

You will find yourself moving closer to identifying your own motivation. Maybe there are areas of life that you feel are your specialty and you feel certain you have something to contribute. Maybe you have had a lot more external life experiences than others and want to share this knowledge with everyone. Whatever your specific reason if you strongly feel that your way is best, your ego is seriously involved in your connection and communication with others. We see the evidence of judging and comparing instead of acceptance and sharing.

How often do you ask for someone's opinion on something that you have the patent on? Do you say, "Well, here's what I would do, no doubt the most efficient way, but what do *you* think would be the best way for you?" Or do you just offer and wait for the advice to be heeded, not for it to be returned? Ego Maturity School lesson for today says this is a 'perk up and take note' moment. When you hear yourself offering advice, even if it is solicited, make sure you do so in the energy of mutual exchange. Offer to assist, but trust that your advice may or may not be the most optimum for your friend. In fact, seeing that no two people are alike, the odds are with you that it is *not* the most optimum method...for *them*.

In my energy healing sessions with clients, I frequently encounter relationships of a difficult nature in their past. As we seek energetically to discover, reconcile and forgive, it becomes obvious that the other people in this person's past situation were always thinking something different than what my client assumed, and acted upon. When they ask me what I think someone was thinking, I say, "I only know this; whatever you think it was, it was something completely different." Given people's different personality traits, soulful lessons they set up and personal and karmic experiences, does it really make any sense that your way would be someone else's way? It rarely is. If you know someone very well, orienting your advice to their nature is helpful, but then only speculative.

It's important to remember that your way is only best for you. You are the only one who knows where your journey will take you. Your intuition works best for you. To empower others by suggesting that they carry the answer within is a lot more effective. It gives them a dose of 'you can do it' and it also takes your suggestion out of the picture, removing any potential blame or setbacks from failing an attempt to perfect *your* way. Once again, let the ego know you are in a maturation process, and that your way may need remodeling, even for you. Maybe it's time to try another way once in awhile.

Let's look briefly at the method of offering advice. Is it given with guilt? Is it offered in a tone of voice that does not invite contradiction? Is it given with the Mr. Know-It-All attitude of unquestionable authority? Or is it offered with genuine concern and personal experience that contributes to a receiver's understanding?

The goal is not to have a plan for every situation, but simply to be aware of how you connect and communicate. Even the most well-intentioned advice may disempower the other person because it unconsciously makes that person feel they *need* help and cannot do it themselves. Years ago I was on the phone with my sister who is younger than me by only 2 years. We had always been close and I enjoyed being the older sister. She looked to me to help her solve her life problems. She would always confide her difficulty of the day and together *we* would try to solve *her* problems. I always thought this process was the dynamic of our relationship until one particular phone call. I was going through what some call the Dark Night of the Soul and was extremely depressed and lethargic. My sister laid out her whole dilemma, and was silent. Normally, I would have dived in and started making suggestions. I said, "Jan, I don't know what to do. But I *do* know that *you* know." The voice on the other end of the line put me to shame. After a pause, she said, "I have waited my whole life to hear you say those words." Needless to say, it changed the dynamic of our relationship from that day forward.

Thinking you are needed may be egically motivated. If you help others because it makes you feel important or needed then it is not empowering to either of you. You don't need to do anything to be valuable; you were created that way. And if someone needs to receive something from you to find the relationship valuable, neither of you are honored. You are sending an unspoken message that says, "I can do it, but obviously you cannot." Awareness of this aspect can tell you more about yourself than the person to whom you are giving advice. If you find that people come to you just for the answers, it may seem like you have no choice. However, the response I finally gave my sister may be the most empowering one, I just shouldn't have waited 40 years to do it.

Lastly, you might consider the frequency of your advice. If it is once every blue moon, which is when there are two full moons in the same month, by the way, and doesn't occur often, you may proceed to the next Ego Maturity lesson. If, however, you find you are offering unsolicited advice several times a day, this lesson is for you. Don't be hard on yourself. Your intention, I am sure, is pure, however, layers of sabotaging ego may be involved. Look at your motivation and your method, take note and decide what you can do about it. For example, if you are offering advice because you really feel that the rest of the human race is pathetically disabled, you may need to do some soul searching. If you are doing it to gain people's favor, that isn't bad, but it isn't empowering either. Why should you need to gain someone's favor? You are a child of the Divine, a radiant light being of love. The purpose of maturing the ego is about having the discipline and awareness to lead and manage your personal unit. Will you be the slave of the unbridled ego, or the product of a conscious decision to allow the Soul Self to guide you?

Engaging in Gossip

This topic makes most people cringe, particularly when they realize how much of their communication is about other people simply for the sake of dredging up something to talk about. When you discuss someone's accomplishments and share in their success, it doesn't feel like gossip. However, when you share the intimate details of their disastrous failure, the ego is alive and pulling the strings. Generally gossip is of a sensationalistic nature. It engages through identifying differences and usually causes harm. It involves rumors and, for the most part, helps direct a negative focus on someone else.

Sometimes it is difficult to avoid gossip. When maturing your ego, the easiest plan is not to begin to engage in it at all. Once gossip begins, it feels like a personal affront to the other speakers, probably your friends, if you take a righteous attitude and stop the flow of communication. The thing to understand is that for the most part, women generally connect by sharing. That is why women seem more prone to gossip, because sharing can become biting or negative and the next thing you know, what began as an honest attempt to connect turned into raking someone over the coals.

You must be vigilant if you know you are susceptible to gossip. If you like to tell stories or you don't want to be left out of a conversation, you could be a carrier of gossip. Decide you are not going to speak poorly of anyone for a particular day or hour, whatever fits. Then when you engage with others in conversation, especially in the coffee room at work, or the family kitchen, pay attention to the conversation's subject. When it looks like it is turning to news of Uncle Remick's latest failed invention or Joe's fight with his wife, take note. It is your turn to act quickly. If plenty of people are present and your absence won't be noted, the easiest thing to do is leave. More than likely, you will be a key player in the communication, and your exit would be rude. Instead of taking up for Remick or Joe, your best tactic is to interject a question or quickly change the subject. You are taking the energy of communication and controlling its path for a moment. You swirl it past the gossip point and plop it out somewhere else. For example, "Yeah, I know about Remick, hey, did you know that last week the Falls Museum opened another exhibit on fossils found right here at the river? I read that it's really neat, you can touch them and everything. Let's all go down together later!" Your enthusiasm turns the conversation quickly into something more fun and less harmful. Everyone will forget about your uncle. They only wanted to connect, and gossip is the path of least resistance; it doesn't require creativity or enthusiasm. It is indeed the lowest path.

And once again, if you do find yourself following along with the group, unable to shift the conversation, don't blame yourself or feel guilty. Just make a mental note of how and when you could have assisted in raising the vibration of the conversation. If your job is to report news for a company, critique an artistic opening, or write a newsletter, know that these venues are avenues for gossip as well. Allow the higher aspects of the events to captivate your audience. No excuses are acceptable for gossip, ever.

If a loved one uses gossip to connect, it is up to you to find another way. Shortening a visit may keep gossip from starting. After all the news blips about both your own lives extinguish, the news may turn to someone else. If someone you know is constantly persuading you to side with them against their enemy to create a common enemy, you may have to hold your ground and say something like, "You know, Valerie really is a kind person. I know you only see this authoritarian side to her, but underneath it is a very sweet child." She may scoff, but she now knows she doesn't have a willing party with whom to gossip. If someone specifically asks you about someone's actions and asks what you think they should do about it, beware. You do not know what they should do; what they are really asking for is a different perspective. And someone who is not personally involved will often be able to assist. If you get personal, and assume the indignant or hurt emotions of the speaker, you will lose your wiser perspective that comes from neutrality.

Remember, every attack is a cry for love. I know that sounds crazy, but underneath all the motivations and confusions is a cry for being loved. From that perspective then, even the worst offender can evoke compassion. Also, the less you engage in gossip, the more trustworthy you will become. The two go together. People will know that you will not gossip about them when you are with someone else. They know you will not allow it and, consequently, they will feel more confident in sharing vulnerabilities with you. Now you are really connecting, heart to genuine heart and the need for gossip is simply gone.

Comparing and Contrasting

We as humans make judgments all day long. It is the way we make decisions that keep us safe and healthy and happy. The concept of comparing and contrasting is what concerns me. Let's look at that concept. Do you remember those dreaded English tests where you had to compare and contrast *Hamlet* with *Romeo and Juliet*? What was the real answer and how did you ever know if you were right? Well, as difficult as this task may have been in high school, comparing and contrasting are quite effortless. For example, do you size up a person as they are walking towards you based on everything you see with your physical eyes: size, weight, status, self-esteem, economic class, intelligence, sexuality and so on? You're comparing them with something, but what? Is it based on something you last saw perhaps in your women's or men's magazines where they show a perfect specimen? Do your criteria come from stereotypes? TV shows? Personal biases? Every part of this scenario involves an unchecked ego. OK, you know the drill; it means we have some work to do.

Do you measure everyone compared to you: to your values? Morals? Intelligence? Good looks? Weight? Level of muscle tone? Hair? Color? Gender? The ego will have you do this to keep you separate. It's not difficult to understand the motives of the ego. It is trying to keep you protected, safe, better than others, the most successful, most handsome, most everything, but isolated for the purpose of meeting needs in a limited resource world. That's the nature of the ego: it wants you to have it all, while others don't. It feels that scarcity is real and tries to convince you that if you don't get it, someone else will. If you don't get rich, there won't be enough and you will go wanting. One problem with the ego is the issue of satisfaction. Do you feel satisfied when you finally obtained something it urged you towards? Have you ever really felt satisfied at all? The nature of the ego dictates that something bigger and better is always out there, somewhere. The motto of the ego is "seek, but do not find."

While living aboard a boat in a coastal town, I would watch massive yachts come into dock while traveling down the coast. One particular slip was big enough for the really big yachts and that's where we boat people often used to go, just out of curiosity. Surprisingly, just when we thought we had seen the biggest and most luxurious yacht known to man, a bigger one would show up two days later, with a helicopter and two cars on deck. The cycle continues on. No matter how wealthy you are, someone is wealthier.

Here is the key. As you measure and compare, try to stop using the eyes of the ego and look through the eyes of the Soul Self. Instead of seeing how you are different, comparing and contrasting, see how you are the same. And I don't mean: he has eyes, I have eyes; he has legs, I have legs; he has a green T-shirt on, I have a green T-shirt. I mean, see how you are exactly the same; see his Higher Self. See that part of him that is the place we all connect, our highest, most divine self. It doesn't necessarily mean it is higher than your head, it means that when you perceive this person, not dwelling on any specific body part or clothing item, what you get is a momentary connection of their Soul Self to yours. Have you ever looked at one of those Magic Eyes pictures, where you see a garbled mess of abstract-looking Jackson Pollack-type art and when your vision relaxes enough, something wonderful takes shape and pops out into 3-D? You can't see it if you strain, in fact, it makes it harder. It is all about relaxing your focus and seeing beyond the picture. That's when you are rewarded with the hidden picture that is always lovely and worth the effort. Once you have experienced a Magic Eye painting, you now know how to regain the vision again, quickly. But you cannot make someone else see it, even if you describe the scene in detail; it just isn't apparent until the correct perception occurs and the picture appears. Well, seeing someone's Higher Self is *just* like seeing a Magic Eye picture!

First of all, you must know that this Higher Self exists. Then you must believe that everyone has one, even people you think are *bad* people. It is our connection to the Divine. It isn't anything like the actual person, it is just part of them, so don't confuse their very visible ego with their highest self. Everyone has a Higher Self and that is ultimately what we all are. If the ego were to take a hike, that is what would remain. Now, to see it (and I use *see* in the mind's-eye way of seeing) the way you *see* in a daydream even though your eyes are closed, you engage another faculty of seeing. It's the way you *see* an image as clearly as if it were happening in front of you while you are reliving a vivid or painful experience.

To experience what I'm describing, walk into the Post Office. You'll see busy people going in and out, smiling or frowning, moving slowly or fast. Pick someone who is coming towards you and whose path you will cross. Then see them with your soul. Do not fixate on their body, their movement, any handicap or garments, only on the area around the eyes. You've probably heard the expression that the eyes are the windows to the soul. In any case, you want to see to *connect*, not just to be curious or a busybody. Imagine a bright area, an energy welling up, a column of incredibly vibrant light or energy, a glowing self. Until you grasp it the first time, you won't know what you are looking for, a lot like the Magic Eye. But ask to see it. Silently ask to see the Higher Self of this person about to cross your path. Then allow yourself to *feel* with your soul, not your emotions, but your soul. The idea is to bypass the comparing/contrasting part of the ritual and connect soul to soul, even if just for a brief moment. A *Course in Miracles* calls this a Holy Encounter and that is what it is. You are connecting the holiest or most divine part of the other person to the holiest, most divine part of you. At that moment, no difference exists between the two of you; you are one in the same. It isn't your bodies, your karma or your history; it's the very substance of your being that has melded with the stranger.

One way to jump-start this experience is to begin with someone you know. Try to think of a time when you were aware of a very tender, loving thing that they did or said. Maybe they didn't even know you were witnessing it, but you saw it and it made an impression on you, possibly because they were vulnerable or available in a way that is not normal for them. Start with this moment of recall. Perhaps it was letting a caterpillar out of the house and placing it gently on the grass when they thought no one was looking. Or maybe it was a time when you caught this person off guard and they confided to you with brutal honesty that made you feel you finally knew them without all their normal barriers. Such fragile moments are glimpses into a gentler, tender self, but do not assume that this Higher Self is weak or powerless. Vulnerability of the ego is often strength to the soul, so when you imagine this Higher Self, do it with an expansive mind because that is what you will perceive.

This approach is the best way to avoid comparing and contrasting, judging and differentiating. The nature of our physical eyes prompts our egos to see what is different. From our very first pre-school experiences we are taught which one is different, the orange or the two apples? We are asked to find the one that does not belong. Subtraction, too, is finding the difference. In this lesson, however, we want to relearn *addition*. Everyone thinks addition is elementary, but it is the core thought process of this ego maturation lesson, and ultimately the soulful lessons too. It's adding together. No matter how many numbers you add, the result is just one sum. *All* equals that one and that is the message. All equals one. The Holy Encounter adds together whereas comparing only limits the lessons. We will discuss this concept of seeing the Higher Self—especially in your own self—later in more detail.

Inconsistent Behavior

Do you give yourself permission to be erratic in behavior? Do you allow external events or hormonal shifts to trigger outbursts of emotional abuse? As often as you are kind and loving, do you also have a side that is mean and cruel? Examine the times you let off steam. Do you have valid excuses for doing so? Are others unwilling participants in your violent eruptions? The thought process necessary here is to determine if your inconsistent behavior is a way to control or unsettle others, or simply an excuse for being emotionally self-indulgent. The inconsistencies of your emotional behavior can undermine your genuine attempts at self-discipline and will continue to make others nervous around you. Even if the occasions are rare, as long as they exist, they pose a threat to both you and those around you.

Examining your motives and your excuses will guide you to where your focus needs to go and will identify your actions that need to be redefined. To simply shrug off the emotional outbursts as part of a fiery personality only leaves the ego sitting firmly in the Captain's chair. As long as the ego knows it has a dependable venue, emerging through its mega-dramatic entrance, it will always have a hook in you. It is up to you to determine what is allowing the hook to remain. Do you always behave erratically, or do you have perfect control at work, leaving the home as the stage for emotional drama; or is it the other way around? Who or what is the reason for that behavior? Do you allow yourself these outbursts only with certain people? Do you profess to love them the most? Do you like to be intimidating? Do you gain something when you are seen as unpredictable? What would being consistent in your behavior even feel like? How would you have to interact with those loved ones to be emotional equals?

The questions help determine the underlying reasons your emotional erratic behavior exists. Then, what to do about it is then determined by what you find. The resources you may have to draw from will range from conscious self-discipline to allowing yourself to acknowledge who you are in relation to this other or others who are affected by your outbursts. As this book will guide you, seeing who you are will help considerably as you correlate these findings into your awareness of who *others* are as well. Your decision to choose peace will bring you face to face with any erratic behavior that challenges that peace.

Credit, Accolades, and Titles

This last section in the Maturation-of-the-Ego process is perhaps a little easier than that last one. It includes all the stereotypical stuff you think of when you imagine an egotistical person. It is a list of questions to trigger an awareness of whether or not you need correction or reassessment. This section is for self-study, not for more analysis of others. Work on it when it feels appropriate.

The assessment questions follow.

1. Does it bug you when someone introduces you with an incorrect title that is lower in hierarchy than your actual one?
2. Do you secretly become jealous when someone talks to you about someone else with great esteem and admiration, especially if they are of the same profession or in a similar category as you?
3. Are you pompous or proud of yourself for deeds you have done that no one knows about?
4. Do you quietly blame someone else or an external situation for your own problems, even if no one is listening?

5. Do you interrupt people while they are relating a story to interject what you just thought of that relates, which of course is about you?

6. Do you want credit for things you feel you personally caused, thought of or created?

7. Does it bug you when either no credit is given or credit that you believe should be yours is given to someone else?

8. Do you listen with a self-absorbed ear for accolades and verbal appreciation at a meeting or gathering hoping they include you?

9. Are you shocked, visibly or secretly, when you are not honored for something you believe you deserve and someone else is honored instead?

10. Can you say, "I'm sorry" and really mean it? Can you say, "I'm sorry" at *all*?

11. Do you introduce others intentionally with a title that can be perceived as *lower* or equal to your own?

12. Do you avoid people who are genuine and kind, because you don't have any tricks that appear to get the best of them?

13. Do you become offended when you are not invited to a meeting that you believe should include you, only because your absence from that meeting makes it seem like you have less power, even though the meeting may really involve things that do not pertain to you?

14. Do you go head to head with people who have more authority than you only to show that you are equally as capable and hope to rope in some power doing it?

15. Do you feel you need to compete with others of your standing in clothing, vehicles, money, home or otherwise?

16. Do you encourage your children to compete, either in sports or in general?

17. Does it disturb you to be proven wrong, and then secretly rationalize until you are never wrong in your own mind?
18. Do you feel slighted when your parent speaks highly of another sibling?

Infinitely more questions could be asked to make you aware that we are living in the material world, as Madonna says, and we have egos to go with it. What you want to ascertain is to what extent you have a full-blown, out-of-control ego-maniac at the controls, and how you can manage whatever level you find yourself. The idea here is to determine how this list of questions applies to you? Does it apply at all? If it does, it means that your ego is more in control than your soul, because these issues are not of the soul. It means that your work is going to include some maturation exercises. It helps especially if you assign someone you know and love—a child, spouse or co-worker—the job of monitoring your errant behavior. For example, you want to stop blaming others or other situations outside your control. Your assigned monitor will hold up a finger or say a particular key word when you need correction. The prearranged signal will be private and subtle, but it will bring to your attention how often you act a certain way, allowing you to make another choice. In this way, you are re-programming old habits and really the ego is just following old habits, responding to stimuli as it has a thousand times before. If you change that response even once, you are creating another pathway in your energy system, as well as your physical neurology, that now exists where nothing existed before. It certainly won't be as worn down as the old familiar path, but it's a start.

Try this experiment with you as your own monitor. At work, watch your responses, the internal ones, to see if they correlate with the words coming out of your mouth. "Oh, I'm *so* happy for you getting that new promotion!" Inside are you saying, "You undeserving lout, the president always liked you better. I never stood a chance with him because I have small breasts! I need to look for another job if people like *you* get promoted above hard-working slaves like *me!*" Assess your internal voice, but don't jump on yourself. Remember, your ego has a job to do and advancement *over* others is part of its goal. But if you take the reins and give them to the Soul Self, what would your internal comments sound like? "She truly has done a creative job and deserves the credit. This promotion has absolutely nothing to do with me, as hard as that is for the ego to believe."

As you monitor yourself, try to see the same situation from the eyes of the Higher Self, that most divine, loving self. It may be difficult sometimes, especially if your core issues are lit up; but because you're reading this book, you must have decided at some point that you wish to make some changes. At some time or another, the power of the ego will be lessened in your life as you journey Home. You can't take it with you, so it may as well be now.

"Do not be afraid of the ego. It depends on your mind, and as you made it by believing in it, so you can dispel it by withdrawing belief from it."

— A Course in Miracles

8 Cultivating a Spiritual Awareness

Children come in uninhibited. As Pablo Picasso said, "Children are born artists. The key is to remain one." Without inhibitions, children are more able to see their inner nature and their unique gifts. It isn't long though, before those very traits that represent their signature are the things that make them feel separate or different when they are ridiculed or embarrassed. The ego works overtime in youth to get everyone on board by insisting that everyone accepts its definition of who they are and then requires them to use the filters it provides to interpret the world.

Even though you come into this life with all kinds of possibilities, eventually all you do is focus on *one*: the *ego*. Since you see your world through the ego lens, you will always get hurt, feel guilty, get punished, or feel unloved or unworthy. These results are all by-products of the ego-centered world. The ego personalizes everything because that is what the ego does; it makes everything be about *me*. What if we were taught that another way exists to view experiences, without processing them through the filter of the ego lens? You might say, "Then we wouldn't be humans." Well, we would be humans; we just wouldn't be the humans that anyone on this planet recognizes.

What if you were taught as a very young infant, by witnessing it in your parents, that when someone is mad at you and yells at you, it has nothing to do with *you*; it is just someone else's fears and phobias being projected onto *you*? (Only your responses belong to you.) What if you were taught how to communicate with others without ever uttering a word, but instead connected to their higher, more receptive centers? What if you were shown how to look at the world as a self-created illusion, that all the world truly is a stage and you could be whatever you choose? You don't have to respond the way the ego insists. What if when anything at all happens, you don't instantly turn it into an egocentric moment, that maybe it has nothing to do with you at all, except that it could be seen as an opportunity for learning or growth? That would be a very different reality.

It would be a world where we wouldn't have to develop twitches, weirdnesses and phobias to cope with a cruel and mean world. Would the world really be cruel and mean if we didn't interpret it that way? What if stuff just happens and it has nothing to do with us? If you can't run the incident through your own perceptions, then it may as well not exist. That's right, if it has nothing to do with *you,* it may not even exist. And if nothing is personal, then maybe the whole egoic world would cease to exist. Is that even possible?

Consider one life, Ivan Ivanovich. Ivan lives like we all do, from moment to moment, responding to experiences with pain and sorrow, anger and delight. He is yelled at by his boss and Ivan grows angry, turns red and either feels guilty inside, like a loser, or superior and condescending. He does it to protect his ego, but do you see what he is doing? He is either putting himself in the inferior position (loser) or the superior one (condescending). He does what the ego does: compares, contrasts and measures up to the competition.

Soon after, Ivan's daughter gets married and he is so happy for her because she is marrying the love of her life. He drinks and dances and makes merry. The ego is smug, "*My* daughter is successful in love." The next day, Ivan trips on a curb and sprains his ankle. It hurts, he curses, and he is late getting to work. His boss yells at him again. Now he is angry and hurting too. Two days later, Ivan goes for a picnic with his lovely wife upon a mountaintop. He surveys the beauty of his land and the forest that surrounds it and the blue sky above him. He is happy and content. Nothing disturbs his fragile ego.

When he returns to work on Monday, Ivan finds he has been passed over by a co-worker for a promotion. The contented ego is now not so contented anymore. The sky is still blue and the forest is still green, but the ego is at war. The ego does not see the beauty of the world when competition provides winners and losers, and Ivan is a loser, well, in his ego's eyes. He tries to speak to his boss about the incident, hoping to assuage his ego, to help it understand a logical reason for his being left behind, but the words don't make sense. At that moment, the ego doesn't speak words, it speaks emotions. Ivan feels more resentment and dislike for his boss than he ever has, making it harder for him to get out of bed the next morning.

Are you beginning to *feel* the cycle of up and down, high then low? That movement is the predictably unpredictable world of the ego. If you live through the eyes of your ego, you will be a slave to this cycle forever. Period. Do you want to get off the merry-go-round? If so, you have one option. You must stop living the ego's way. There is no change, yet constant change; there is no joy, but fleeting joy; there is no peace that is eternal. You are too familiar with Ivan's story. It's always up, down, sad, happy, joyful, angry, depressed, peaceful, high, low. You think that even though everyone follows this pattern, *you* will be the one to find some way to hang on to happiness. You can even take it with you; you can plan for it in old age. You think that if this or that illusory thing is procured or an experience happens, then you will be assured happiness for the rest of your life.

Your cells know that I am describing the cycle that has continued since the beginning of time, but your brain says, "Maybe not me. If I can just finish this degree, or if I can just get this one job or mate or face lift, or whatever." But you know the cycle is imprinted in you as surely as the need to survive.

Why then are you reading this? You must also know that a way out of the endless cycle of life and death is indeed possible, because that is essentially what it is: it is life and death, figuratively and literally. Life is found through one opening, and death through another. Stop bashing your head ceaselessly against a doorway that just leads you right back into the cycle of death again and again. Turn aside and walk peaceably to the doorway marked, "Spirits enter here." That means the ego must remain behind. Hallelujah!

Here's how it works. You identify what is the ego: *the ego is everything that is not love and joy.* That means anything that does not have love and joy as its end result is born of the ego. Here's an example: conflict. Love is not the result of conflict and conflict does not generate love. It's very easy to see where conflict comes from.

Thoughts of worthlessness when thinking of one's life, images of inferiority while looking in the mirror, feelings of lacking when comparing your security to your neighbor's are all emotions created by the ego.

What generates love? Feelings of wanting to share with someone less fortunate (as long as those feelings are not based on superiority, but joy and love), forgiveness, truly loving selflessly, following your heart and quitting your job, opening your own business, if that is your joy, spinning around naked under the moonlight in a clear mountain lake all generate joy. Now, look at your own life. What do you love to do? What generates love and joy for you? It is different for everyone. You see, you are the "...beginner of this vile fray" as the quote goes from Romeo and Juliet. You created it, so *what brings you joy will be your way out.* That is your own private doorway to another reality. It is really that easy.

You must change the way you see. You must begin to look with your inner vision, not your body's eyes. Everything you see with your eyeballs is deluding you, so look instead through the eyes of your spirit. And how, prey tell, do you do that?

Before we can begin to see, we must learn to respond differently, which is almost as difficult as learning to see out of eyes that we are not aware of. It is all about flipping everything. When someone says something to you that instantly lights up your ego, it hurts. It sends your emotional self on a roller coaster ride over which it has no control. Here's an example, you pride yourself on being considerate, or trying the best you can. However, you allow others to sometimes take advantage of you or you put them first, leaving what is left for you. You call it considerate, I call it martyrdom. Time and time again, you have taken a smaller portion or missed out on fun experiences because you believe you stand aside, allowing others to have more at your expense. Let's say, the one person you have come to resent the most—the one taking advantage of you, or teaching you it does not empower anyone to be a martyr—says something like, "Well, Margaret doesn't need any of this stuff, she has always been the first to take when anything comes around." Your blood pressure rises. You think, "After *all* the sacrifice, this is what others think of me?" You are ready to list every act of sacrifice you have made for the past 3 years in chronological order to set the record straight if you need to.

Is any of this real? Is anything helping you find your doorway out, and off this mad farm? Is anything generating love and joy? It is not, therefore, it must be ego created. So instead of responding with the tried and true (truly tried for virtually ever), let's try the New School approach. Acknowledge the ego is at work, making you feel like *less,* while she feels like *more.* Realize that no one is asking you to process this comment through you. It is a reflection of this woman's own self-centered, ungiving nature which truly has nothing whatsoever to do with you. If you want to engage the ego, respond. Then you will continue the Ivan Ivanovich story: up, down, high, low, happy, sad until the end of time.

Do you want to find your way out? Go about your life, keep giving if it makes you happy, receiving if it brings you joy. Stay in experiences that generate love and joy. You say, "What if I have no control?" You are not being forced to have a certain response. Choose a *different* response. In *every* situation, there will be a decision that will generate love and joy, or a different one that will not. Always choose the one that generates love and joy. That is your only criteria.

Let's take another example. What if you are being mugged or raped or beaten? The ego would have you be indignant or afraid or angry, and you would feel justified. So, go ahead, feel justified. Is it a good enough feeling that you would want to stay in the cycle of life and death forever just to feel justified? It's your world. What other options do you have? First of all, if you don't carry victim energy, which means you believe you have no control over your reality, the probability of being accosted is reduced to almost nothing. But let's say, you are being accosted. What in the world could possibly bring you joy and love right now? Everything in your old way of thinking says nothing will, but it is your body being accosted; you do not have to allow someone to accost your soul. So you take your energy into your Highest Self, you speak to the Higher Self of the accoster. You see the Highest Self of this damaged ego, and you allow yourself to find a way to think of someone you love or who loves you or who loves them. Is that impossible? Is that unorthodox? Do you feel indignant? It is your choice.

I'm reminded of a Tibetan monk I went to hear speak on forgiveness who had spent 30 years in prison being tortured. He said for years he prayed for death. He was so undernourished he tried to eat the leather on his shoes, and watched while others came and went or came in and received the mercy of death. At some point in his imprisonment, he chose to rise above his predicament and began to see his oppressors in a loving way. Eventually, he came to forgive them. So when he spoke of forgiveness, I listened. He was still tortured, but he said it did not carry the heaviness of victimhood because he had chosen another response. They had no control over him, since forgiveness was in his heart. He also explained to us that it changed the nature of his entire life. After that experience he was actually able to *live* his tenants and share them with others in a kind and loving way. When things happen to you, you have two choices: One will generate love and joy and one will not. One opens a door to peaceful living and the other takes you right back to start the endless cycle again.

Here's another example. You have a desire to live with a person you love very much. You also know that if you follow this course, without an approved certificate from the local government office or religious institution, your parents will be unhappy with you. You are not sure you are ready to commit your life to this other person just yet. You want to see more aspects of this person, so you go ahead and move in. Now, you are faced with a decision. Do you tell your parents, do you lie, do you avoid the subject, or do you keep your now vacated apartment for appearances? The answer is up to you. It is whichever one will bring you the most joy and love. If you know that the truth will make you the happiest, then by all means, tell the truth. But if you know that your parents are entrenched in the Old School and would feel offended and saddened, and it would create a gap between you, and you value your relationship at any cost, then do whatever you need to do that would make you the happiest. But don't dilute the decision with guilt. If you have decided it brings you peace, then allow that decision to be enough. Be creative. Let yourself feel the outcome of joy and love.

This repeating process is like a Hamster Wheel. Let's look at some specific examples of how we again and again can choose, through our thoughts and actions, how to slow it down and step quietly off.

The Hamster Wheel

The hamster wheel is a metaphor for the repetitious life of the ego-centered world that does not allow us to leave the cage for freedom, or for anything different at all. It only keeps us spinning around, again and again, perpetuating the game. But what happens when you want to get off? Who has the key to slow it down? Who put you there in the first place? Why can't you just stop? There is no reason other than we have bought into an illusion that exists only in our collective minds so no one gets off; we all continue to play the ego game and spend our well earned energy here and nowhere else.

Let's say that you want to get off the hamster wheel. You want to experience peace, freedom, and something other than repetition. You truly want to stop the cycle of life and death. You don't want to play this game anymore. A way out does exist, and it is under your control. It is in altering the nature of your responses. It is *choosing* a different response other than the one the ego has scripted for you. Remember, the ego promotes separation, competition, anger, frustration, greed, envy and an insatiable appetite for self, not self-worth though, only self (as in self-destruction). *A Course in Miracles* states,

> *Every response you make is determined by what you think you are, and what you want to be is what*

you think you are. Therefore, what you want to be
determines every response you make.

So the responses that we have to the experiences of this world in turn generate more responses of this world. That means we produce ego responses, like being angry or outraged when we perceive that someone has hurt us. We respond with suffering when we feel pain, resentment when we feel used, heartbreak when someone stops having lust for us, and grief when someone we love leaves their body.

These responses are all normal in the sense that you have come to accept an insane world as normal. However, you're trying to get off the hamster wheel. To do that you choose a response *not* of this world, but from a higher place, *your* Highest Self, in fact. But what does that mean? Do I **not** get mad when someone runs over my dog intentionally because she barked last night? Do I **not** get sad when someone leaves me for another realm by taking their own life? Do I **not** feel glad when someone who I think deserves it gets in trouble? That is exactly what it means. Before the ego steps in you look to your Higher Self for a response, and you choose another reaction. You find understanding that comes from peace, joy, forgiveness and love which are emotions that are *not* from this world. Even though they exist in this world, they come from a higher plane of existence. You must choose from that menu if you want to leave the hamster restaurant. You choose, hamster pellets or out-of-this world fare!

Each time you choose a response from a different category, one that comes from love, forgiveness and joy, you slow the hamster wheel and eventually get off. Each time you choose a response that creates more separation and negativity, you tie yourself tighter onto the wheel. It's that simple? It's that hard. Try for *one* different reaction today. You will see how engrained the preprogrammed responses are and how much conscious effort it takes to even think of trying something else, much less investigating your options.

Let's run over a few more examples. What's your most logical (logical in an insane world, don't forget) reaction to the following situation? Your daughter comes home having failed a standardized educational test for her grade. She is pretty upset because her teacher has made her feel like an incapable loser. For teachers, this testing validates their world; for your daughter, it begins the world of her against them (ego=separation, competition, remember?). What is your first reaction? You are angry, internally upset that your daughter may not be any brighter than you, or not as bright as you were hoping, as measured by some assumedly bright people somewhere who write standardized tests. Looking for some external entity to blame, you ask what she was doing while taking the test. You suspect drugs or inattentive behavior or someone goofing off with her. Someone must be to blame (more of the 'you against them' story). You're still in the ego response, stuck in the hamster wheel forever. What if you told her she was grounded, and punished her for her irreversible test score that will mar her forever; will that help her to be more serious next year? No. What if you said you'd speak to her father who would deduct allowance money to demonstrate he is not proud of this failure? You're still looking at infinity in Hamsterville. She *must* be taught that it's a dog-eat-dog world out there, and to be labeled a poor student, a failure from this young age, will definitely detract from her chances at success. All these reactions are ego-based. Natural, sure, because they are familiar, but they are not generated from love or forgiveness, understanding or joy.

Here's another possible response. Your daughter comes home with a note from her teacher saying she has failed her standardized test for her grade. You walk over to her and hug her and tell her how much you love her. You explain that there will be many tests in this world; and the least important are standardized tests from her elementary school. You assure her that she is being prepared through love and forgiveness for the really big tests of life. Then you go for ice cream. Who is going to make her feel like a loser? It won't be you, and you are her role model. You carry more clout than anyone, and you love her. Hamster wheel, good-bye!

Your friends may say you are too easy and that your soft reaction will cause her to not take next year's tests seriously. That is more ego trying to tell us that its institutions are sacrosanct, that success comes from societally accepted methods. Have you ever met an older person who is contemplating the nature of their life? Have you ever seen a movie where a wise person is dying, sharing with the viewing audience all the really important things in life? Are they ever about passing the standardized tests in 4th grade? Are they ever about getting straight As in school? Most people don't even remember much about school, at least not without a stomach ache. People who feel successful, who are connecting to that spiritual (non-egoic) side of themselves, carry the mark of being loved, of having loved, of sharing or helping, of being kind when it was important. Their mark reflects being courageous, facing fears, protecting vulnerable hearts, acting selflessly without a moment's hesitation, and never giving up on themselves. Is there some part of this that could have happened or failed to happen if the participant did or did not pass a certain grade school test?

What about another response? Remember, if it comes from love, joy and forgiveness, it takes you off the hamster wheel. This one is harder. You are going to spend Christmas without your children for the first time ever. They will celebrate with their father, and if that weren't hard enough, your ex has a significant other who will now be present too. Where do your thoughts go? Have you already trashed this innocent person who is beginning a relationship with your previous love? Do you feel jealous? Do you feel left out, lonely, betrayed? Your children are spending a special occasion not only with someone you don't even know, but with someone you don't even like. Then your children come

home raving about how much fun they had with your ex-spouse
and the newcomer. Your first instinct might be to make them
shut up about the whole affair, because you can't bear to hear
about it. You are comparing yourself to the other. You are feeling
left out and second hand, maybe betrayed by *your* children that
they would like someone you have already determined was an
enemy. What next?

The task ahead means having different responses to *everything*:
every single thing, little and big. But you can just start with one
day, one experience.

You do *not* need to fall into the trap of being a victim, or
feeling betrayed, or angry. You co-created this moment for a
learning experience of huge magnitude. Ask for guidance and
turn your inquiries inward. Look for forgiveness, for genuine
love, not only for the other, but also for yourself. Do not allow
yourself to feel like a victim or you will be one. And you are not.
The only way off this eternal wheel of suffering is to hold the
ego at bay. It is howling at the door, but try instead to hear the
still, small voice within. What do you hear? A message is there
expressly for you. Maybe it says you are looking for a way to put
the past behind you and move on in your own life. Maybe it says
your children are free to have joy, and it doesn't have to be at your
expense; it can be *with* you. Maybe it says you are ready to honor
yourself and are ready to invite the perfect mate into your life. Are
your children there to pry open your rusted-shut heart to allow
your to embrace the possibility that they may have a new parent
in addition to you? Can you actually step out of your hurt and
bruised ego and hug your children in genuine love and be happy
that they find joy with someone else? The message is that who
you are is not dependant upon anyone else, or anyone else's love.
There could be a million words for a million different people.
This story of ego-betrayal is as old as time, and the ego tosses it
at us when we least suspect it. It is part of the insanity of life, but
we always run right into the trap, every time, like Pavlov's dogs.

But this time you are going to try a higher response. And as you do this, the ego owns you less and less. You are taking your power back and embracing your Highest Self. What does that mean? It means that your ego self is diminishing its control and power over you, and your higher, more spiritual nature is growing and gaining in power and control.

Try these scenarios: you smash your finger with a hammer, get paint on your new outfit, discover that your computer lost years worth of valuable data, drop a special wine glass, break your leg just before a long awaited trip to Europe. All these have such common responses that you feel them without even skipping a heartbeat. But do you feel the higher, soulful response? Do you hear yourself consoling your finger, saying it lives under a higher set of rules and doesn't need to hurt if it doesn't want to? Do you hear yourself stepping away from the computer, readjusting priorities and taking the kids to the park with the dog? Do you see yourself beginning the project you have always wanted to do but never had the time while everyone else is in Europe? Perhaps you can get a massage and a facial while they're gone too! These responses stem from love, forgiveness and joy, and not just for others; it's love and forgiveness and joy for yourself too!

The ego would tell you that having love for yourself is self-love and egotistical. It would tell you it is prideful to indulge in or be proud of yourself. But this type of logic is diametrically opposed to Truth. It says that who you are is defective and sinful. It perpetuates this misperception for its own existence; therefore, you should be repentant and humble. However, in Truth, you are Divine. And as a divine being, loving yourself is what is expected, because by loving what you are, you give credence to your God-created Self and the God-created Self of others. Remember, it is not about pumping up the ego and inflating it even more, creating yet more division between you and others; it is about rejoicing together in our Divine Natures. As *A Course in Miracles* says, "To accept yourself as God created you cannot be arrogance because it is the denial of arrogance. To accept your littleness is arrogant because it means that you believe your evaluation of yourself is truer than God's."

Who you are *is* love. How could you yourself be exempt from the love you emanate? To make a conscious choice to change your responses, or at least recognize when they come from love and when they come from fear, you deeply challenge the power your ego holds over your world.

"Where God is, there are you." – A Course in Miracles

9 God and Religion

God, Responsibility and Assistance

If the world were *without* the concept of an almighty God, capable of all, fully equipped with armies of angels and every conceivable method of miracles, we would be better off. I really believe that. I think that this man-created image of God, or the Old Testament version of God, has kept us fully stagnant in the victim mentality. If God is so all-powerful, why is He silent in my life? How could He let this terrible thing happen in someone else's life? How could so much pain and abuse be rampant in this world? Why doesn't He save me? That is the key. Why doesn't Mister God along with Mister and Missus Santa Clause come and save me from this complex world of suffering? Why can't I just have one little miracle, just this once, because I don't know how to get out of this predicament. I cannot handle what I am going through. I cannot suffer heartbreak any longer. These thoughts and questions provide a glimpse into the back of our minds where this wild card called God resides.

Unfortunately, this man-created image of *God* is exactly that, an image of an omnipotent God created in the image of *man* for the purposes of control and manipulation, along with a myriad of other reasons. But the bottom line is, as long as we believe that we can draw this wild card, we never really play like we were completely responsible. We hope that if we are good enough, whatever that means, depending upon the religious group we subscribe to, that God will manifest Himself at just the perfect time to make all the bad things go away. This type of thinking may not even be conscious. If you look at the history of humanity, you see much abuse and many mis-deeds done in the name of this Almighty God. Even if we look just at the last 1000 years, we see the Inquisition, the Crusades, the Holocaust, the witch hunts, healers killed in the name of God because they were threatening the life support of the church. We see people still being excommunicated from their churches, people being shunned, marked, disgraced, killed, tortured, maimed, ripped in half, raped, and disemboweled. We see them with their heads shaven, tattooed with death numbers, removed from their countries, humiliated…all in the name of someone's God.

Now, it seems to me we have a problem. If we really are waiting on this miracle dispensing God to come save us, do we really want to be saved by a vengeful, wrathful, scary entity the likes of which we have probably encountered at some point along our soul's journey? Many people say they are way beyond the Old Testament version of God and now believe in a loving, supportive Divine Being, ready and willing to assist us as we grow towards our Highest Self. I believe that. I think that, consciously, we all believe that. But I know in almost every energy healing session I have held some connection still exists to this scary character we at some point gave power over us. I believe that there is a catch-22 about playing the God card. We may believe that God is mister miracle man, but in using that card, we may be awakening a force that may turn on us instead of bestow miracles on us.

If you had your arms ripped apart and your last memories were those of church men sent from God telling you that you were an unforgivable sinner and heading to hell, while you were processing that message, between the screams of terror and indescribable pain, you just *may* have put some pretty strong beliefs into your energy system. No doubt, those beliefs came in handy in later lives, so you never upset anyone in the church or did anything you weren't supposed to do (you knew your very life depended on it). However, the horrid incident also jaded your belief in a loving, supportive God. So now you say you are beyond that old God, and very well you may be; but I suggest that threads of the Old Testament God are still unraveling somewhere inside your subconscious mind.

The beliefs that you hold unconsciously keep you in old behavior patterns and prevent you from having total trust or faith. The old belief in your man-made God also keeps you feeling it is your fault if miracles don't happen to you. This belief keeps you sitting right on the fence, not really wanting to awaken the sleeping giant, fearing how He will wake up, and yet wanting desperately to be saved, to be held and loved by the creator of all, to be loved unconditionally, to have all your sins wiped away and to feel safe.

Let me ask this question. What would the Creator of All create as an expression of itself? Would it be a human body limited by time, space and matter, filled with puss and excrement, that decays and dies in a filthy pile of stinking rot? Or would it be a divine light being that never changes, has no limitations of any kind, material or otherwise, and is the manifestation of love and peace? Which one sounds like it would be man-created and which one Divinely created?

Responsibility

This is where responsibility comes in. If I were to suggest that you forget the Old Testament version of God, you'd reply that you already had. So that isn't the way. If I were to say, "Imagine that God is not a person." God, or as I prefer to call this entity, the Divine, is rather an energy. The Divine is the life-force energy that created All, and we all know that. But what does that knowledge mean to you, still wanting a miracle and wanting to be saved? It means that you are completely capable of saving yourself. It means that you were created with creative life-force energy which, in turn, means the attributes of this Divine energy stream, are in you too. In other words, the Creator of All that has enlivened the universe has created us with this grand energy of unconditional love, the highest of all vibrations. That Creator infused us, all Its creations, with Itself, and that means, It filled us with everything It is. As the saying goes, like father, like son; the apple doesn't fall far from the tree. Therefore, if you have been waiting for someone *outside* yourself to come and save you, to make you whole, to redeem you, to wash you clean, to forgive you, I am here to suggest that no one is out there waiting to save you. We are all gods, so what are you waiting on? And what do you need saving from? Would God need you to save Him? From what? Save Him from the flood that He supposedly created, sins that man created, misperceptions that man misinterpreted? If you knew you were God, how would you live your life differently?

It's similar to an example I often give to my clients trying to help them understand what they are. Imagine you were home one day and received a caller at the door. Upon opening the door, you discovered that you were being served papers requiring you to contact this particular lawyer. After doing that, you found out that you were the sole heir to the Rockefeller fortune. Your life would certainly change. What I am suggesting is that knowing that you were created in the True likeness of God—not in the likeness of a man-created god—you have as your birthright access to universal power, divine wisdom, unconditional love, unlimited blessings *and* miracles, intuition, guidance, support and essentially everything you could ever want. Now, would you wait for a miracle from some sleeping giant-God that you fear?

No. You would begin to create your life just as you would prefer to live.

Let me give you another thought. If you can fathom that the Divine is not a two-legged mammal with supernatural powers, can you imagine that the Divine is a vibration of energy? This vibration is only that, a strong unwavering energy signal of unconditional love. And before I go on, let me say that unconditional love is not something we understand easily. I was working with a young woman some time ago and asked her if she understood the concept of unconditional love. Before I could explain, at least in theory, she said, "Yes, I am very familiar with it, I have two boys I love that way." I then asked her, "If your oldest boy murdered your youngest boy, would you still love that oldest boy the same as you do now?" She paused and said, "Oh, I see what you mean. Yes, that would be very hard...almost impossible." Almost impossible is what unconditional love is, but that is the vibration of the Divine.

Unconditional love is when you are loved *no matter* what you do, what you wear or don't wear, who you marry, what you eat on Fridays or on the Sabbath, whether or not you have the appropriate garments or skull cap for your religion, whether or not you have a religion at all. Unconditional love means that mass murders are loved *exactly* the same as you are! That thought sets you back a minute, doesn't it? This love is the love of the Divine; it is essentially the vibration of the Divine. Now if you wanted to spend time with the Divine, the Creator of the Universe, do you think you would be kept from it? Not at all, however, you must vibrate with unconditional love to be together. Divinity cannot come down into our vibrations of anger and hatred, resentment and frustration; it can only be what it is, which is unconditional love. Think of the Divine, or God, or Christ Consciousness, or the Universe, or whatever you like to call it, as a river. It is a river of love that is constantly flowing. It is not judging who can or cannot partake of its healing waters. It simply flows. It brings life and rejuvenation to all who touch it. It cools with eternal peace. It strengthens with the constancy of its flow. It exists and it is God. Our bodies are three fourths water, so wouldn't it feel natural to return to this source? Or perhaps, better stated, wouldn't it feel better to realize we are made from God water?

The essence of this journey is the recognition that you are already God; you are not on a journey seeking God somewhere else. When you release all the things that are *not* God, what remains is your own godliness.

Responsibility, therefore, is a lesson you master on your journey Home. Standing up from the side of the road, realizing no one is going to come by to pick you up, you finally start to assess and make decisions about where to go next. Which way is the closest town? How much food and water do you have? Do you have a phone? Is there someone you can you call for help? You have waited 2 days and no one is coming. No one even knows you are stranded, and it is up to you to get home yourself. If you believed this premise, two things would happen. One, you can stop believing in a God that never satisfies and is eternally silent and two, you would start channeling your own divine resources into assisting yourself.

Assistance

If you are a divine creature, created by a living, loving, creative life being, you are entirely more capable than you know. You are headed to the same place that we all are eventually, and that place is Home. So why not help each other? If you really knew you were loved the same by God, and that you were a mini-replica of Divinity, would you need anyone or anything outside yourself to show you God? No, it would be ridiculous. You would say, "thank you," but I have an excellent vantage point here because it is *in* me. Would you give away your power to institutions that tell you what you must do or not do, wear or not wear, eat or not eat to be loved by God? No, you would know in the cells of your re-remembered being that you have always been loved by God and always will be; it's your birthright. Would you still need help once in awhile when you forget this Truth? Yes.

And that is what assistance is *all* about. Assistance always comes whether you ask for it or not, but why not ask and speed up the delivery process? Asking for assistance and then leaving an open-ended expectation lets you receive help in ways you may not have expected.

Who do you ask? When do you ask? All of us traveling together on this journey Home would love to help. Ask someone you know. Ask someone you don't know. Once while traveling alone, my vision was not clear enough to read the top line of an airline monitor, which held my flight information. I couldn't find anything to stand on to be able to see it better. Finally I stopped a man and asked if he could read the top line to me. He was most gracious and I was very grateful. It was a positive experience for us both. I allowed myself to receive help and he got to give it.

All sorts of non-physical guides and helpers are available, and we will talk about them in detail later. Their job is to monitor the energy waves that carry distress calls, and then respond. You may think no one hears, but remember, you are Divine yourself, so why wouldn't you be heard? Many processes may work for you personally and you can connect daily: meditation, yoga, or prayer. Using any of them helps you connect with others of a high frequency, allowing you to compare notes, get feedback, and most of all, get wisdom and guidance about whatever troubles you perceive. Those people that loved you while they were in a physical body (a parent, grandparent, aunt, etc.) may now reside in spirit form, and they watch and wait to help. Ask them.

Creatures and powers of the upper and lower worlds that are found through Shamanic journeying can also guide and assist. Remember, they do not save, but they do guide. Powers of the forest, the sea, wild creatures, power animals, the desert, and the sky can be called upon to embrace your call for help. Assistance may come through the power of astrology, and by understanding your own spiritual natal map and making sense of it. You could use cards and stones, gems and crystals, mantras and affirmations. Whatever power you call upon may empower or disempower you, however you choose to use it. You are a creation-filled being, which means you can embody anything with power. It's the same with pills and medicine. If you empower them with your life power, they can help you heal, but if you do not, they are just simple tablets with no assistance to give.

Books and authors that speak to you guide and assist you along the journey. You may also seek guidance from spiritual healers, Ascended Masters, Buddhas, Bodhisattvas, counselors, guides and speakers. Many workshops and seminars are geared to help you find your way Home. Movies, theatre productions, sculptures, fine art, and poetry also have much to offer through symbolism, metaphors and inspiration along your journey. Children's books, fairy tales, old television programs, archetypes and fables all hold symbolic themes that guide you, consciously or not, Homeward. You will also find radio programs and internet web pages designed to share thoughts and ideas that inspire and guide. The list is limitless. The message is, you are not alone. We are all traveling, we are all Gods, we are all loved and no one is going to come save us except ourselves. And then, and only then, do we discover we never needed saving at all.

How Does Religion Fit into the Spiritual Journey?

I work with many people who are in the individuating phase of their journey and they invariably ask me how they can comprehend what religion has to offer while seeking a higher spiritual connection. Frequently, by the time someone has individuated, or is in the process of separating from a group, they encounter so many negative experiences they just want to forget the journey and turn back around towards a place of familiarity. This experience occurs with any tribe.

A tribe is a unit held together by a bond, and that bond in a religion is the set of beliefs. So when someone starts to push the boundaries of those beliefs, the core of the tribe responds in kind by pushing back. That pushing back often feels personal, as if you were being picked on for questioning authority. And you are; such is the nature of the tribe. If the tribe allows everyone to question what the tribe stands for, then it would not remain a strong tribe for long. The very nature of a tribe is to be a structural support group for those in need. If the structure is weak or wobbly, those who need a strong support will not feel secure. You see, it's not really personal at all, yet as part of our growth experience, it seems we *all* go through some sort of individuation process, whether it's from an organized religion, a family group, an institution or a gang.

The element that is changing in the tribe is *you*, not them. They are right where they are for a reason; it's where they feel they need to be. The structure, the rules, the boundaries give them the protection and direction they need. Somewhere along your journey you have belonged to any number of tribes of one sort or another. Others members are there because it is part of their journey. So just because you might be changing or outgrowing those boundaries does not mean that anyone else from the group is going to stand up and say, "Hoorah, our brother here is moving on, blessings and good luck." In fact, they can say any number of things, but they are *not* allowed to utter those words. If someone does, in quiet, they are probably at some stage of individuating themselves.

You may feel some sense of resentment, something akin to, "I have given that group everything and have been such a vital player, and *this* is how I am treated when I choose to move on." In fact, the *more* vital a player you were, the more they will try not to lose you. If you were a slaggart, only half-heartedly giving your time and energy to the group, they might be happy to see you move on. Any resentment you feel is well founded. Remember, everyone is only being who they are at the time and place they occupy along their journey.

The following entry comes from Thoreau's journal in 1850 and describes one who has individuated from his tribe.

> *I do not prefer one religion or philosophy to another.*
> *I have no sympathy with the bigotry and ignorance*
> *which make transient and partial and puerile*
> *distinctions between one man's faith or form of*
> *faith and another's, – as Christian and heathen.*
> *I pray to be delivered from narrowness, partiality,*
> *exaggeration, bigotry. To the philosopher all sects, all*
> *nations, are alike. I like Brahma, Hari, Buddha,*
> *the Great Spirit, as well as God.*

The fingerprint of the ego is present in religion as in every other institution on Earth. Anything that separates, creates guilt, inflicts punishment or judgment and openly promotes some people over others is the handiwork of the ego, not of God.

Many of my clients ask me how they can make sense of all the promises and oaths they took in their various religions. I say, if they lose their value in your mind because you have come to some other understanding, that is how much value they still possess. Remember, this illusion has been created by your mind; you can recreate it or amend it similarly. It is like a curse. If someone curses you and you believe they have the power to do it, you will take it on as if it were yours and you own it. This ownership makes the curse *real*. If you don't believe for one minute that that person could curse a flea, you allow the energy of the curse to just slide off your back. It is the same with an oath, vow or promise. How many of us have made promises somewhere along our lives to love someone "till death do us part," only to become disillusioned a few painful years later and divorce them? Most of us have, according to statistics.

The spirit has one purpose in mind and that is to return you to your rightful place, as a Divine Being with the architect of this universe. Naturally, you are going to experience many changes and evolve into the being who is capable of returning. As part of that journey, you are going to encounter experiences where you believe in something with every fiber of your being, only to later move to another belief system. Part of that experience is to completely dedicate your efforts to something simply to see if the results are effective. It is the intensity that you desire. You must know if the path you've chosen leads Home. Sometimes if you don't try hard enough, you wonder, "Was that the way?" But you didn't push on the door hard enough or try another entrance around back. When you concentrate all your efforts in one frontal assault, you will forever know if that was or was not the way. That approach has more value than you know. It helps dissolve the resentment when you know that your experience of giving it your all, was actually the place you needed to be, doing what you needed to be doing as part of your journey.

A close friend of mine recently dealt with this exact issue. She was devoutly religious, but had been having thoughts for sometime that her church confined her. She felt like she was living two lives: one for her community and religion, and the other inside herself. Her spirit was moving on and did not want to wait. At the same time, her relationship with her husband of 30 years had lost all sense of purpose or feelings of enjoyment. In every fiber of her being, she felt that someone else was out there who could appreciate her unconfined spirit and she longed to be with him. However, divorce was out of the question in her religion. She believed that if she were to divorce, she would be ostracized, her family would disown her, her community would label her, and so on.

Nonetheless, the love she felt in her heart for this unknown man spurred her on to take action. She knew that she was in for a lot of heartache if she divorced her husband, both very active in their church, but what was really happening here? The way I see it is her spirit wanted to take her Home to that place of unconditional love and joy. She wasn't really conscious about her spirit's desire; she just wanted to be happy and adored. How does the spirit encourage her to go Home? It uses her deep desire to be wholly loved to move her into action, to step out of her stifling relationship. I see the core issue in this way. She does not believe (in her core-belief self) that she is lovable. How do you return to love when it doesn't feel like Home? How do you attract the most loving man in the world when you cannot receive love? Well, something had to happen that was big enough to say to her, "I am always loved and always will be, and what others think of me is their business."

What had to happen? She could have had an epiphany. That would have been easy. Or she could have chosen most common human selection, and that would be to take the hard road. She would announce that she no longer loved her husband, ask for a divorce from the church, deal with everything from anger to humiliation by all sorts of people she thought loved her and several time bubbles later, she would realize who she is. She would know that her *real* essence is loved by the Divine, that she is in fact, a Divine Being. Eventually, we *all* will realize this Truth.

If this realization comes to her, and if she can stay true to herself, she will become this lovable being and then, guess who she will attract? It will no doubt be the loving guy she dreams about. The process gives her the option to either choose 'A' and go Home or choose 'B' and return to the Hamster Wheel. I hear the food is very constant on the Hamster Wheel. She has forever. The soul, however, looks at experiences as opportunities for growth. See where the soul is guiding you. It is not a question of being right or wrong. It is about using the experience to move you to a higher vibration, a Higher Self.

I picture organized religion as a set of stairs leading to a platform. Those stairs can represent teachings of morality, ethics, values, or guidelines, principles with a scope larger than any one person. They are something to grow towards. Finally when you reach the top of this platform, your journey is solo. Except this is where the church community does not agree. They want to take you Home, and you must pay a price in the form of time, commitment, money, or handing over of personal power, will or energy. The big shock is, no one can get you there. It is a private journey the rest of the way because it is internal.

The following words are taken from a piece called *Charge of the Goddess* and have touched my heart a thousand times. The message is expressed more eloquently than I ever could.

> *I, who am the beauty of the green earth and the white moon among the stars and the mysteries of the waters, I call upon your soul to arise and come unto me. For I am the soul of nature that gives life to the universe. From me all things proceed and unto me they must return. Let my worship be in the heart that rejoices, for behold all acts of love and pleasure are my rituals. Let there be beauty and strength, power and compassion, honor and humility, mirth and reverence within you.* ***And you who seek to know me, know that your seeking and yearning will avail you not, unless you know the mystery, for if that which you seek you find not within yourself, you will never find it without.*** *For behold I have been with you from the beginning and I am that which is attained at the end of desire.*

The bottom line is, the Divine resides in you. It always has, and always will. So we often spend a great deal of time, spinning our wheels looking everywhere *but* there, because we don't believe that is possible at all. Many people take advantage of our wheel spinning to acquire our power, will and sometimes money and material possessions to attempt to help us get there, when *there* is simply a connection to God within us all. We came with that connection, we have always been wired that way. Some may point the way, some people's words may inspire, and others may temporarily accompany us, but in the end, we must walk that path alone.

So don't throw the baby out with the bathwater. If there are some teachings, some places you consider sacred, some understandings that give you strength, some icons that empower you, then integrate them into your journey, but know that the journey is yours alone. You must walk it, or rather rediscover it, yourself. Don't let anyone ever tell you that you're not on the right path. They don't have your assignment and don't know where your path leads you along the way. There are as many ways back to the Divine as there are living beings that exist.

"What is peculiar in the life of a man consists not in his obedience, but his opposition, to his instincts. In one direction or another he strives to live a supernatural life."

— Henry David Thoreau

10 Making Room for Change: Removing the Mask

Reprogramming Sensations

Part of the difficulty of growing is moving through old behavior patterns. They are familiar and comfortable, but often they limit growth. You feel the desire to include more expansive beliefs or allow for infinite blessings, but old behaviors or old programming keep the fences firmly in place. These patterns may involve emotional responses, triggers for emotions such as pain, grief, or anxiety, and expectations caused by certain stimuli. When the mind has a new understanding of something, the body must be updated to accommodate that new understanding or it attempts to respond in old ways. As we have discussed, the body is an empty vessel incapable of making decisions or directing your life, but it holds neurological memories of repetitive thoughts or actions. The mind is doing the work, so the mind needs to be involved in reprogramming.

One of life's most common sensations is pain and you have already programmed many things that cause you pain. They range from physical things (stubbing your big toe), to mental things (judging yourself a loser), to emotional things (expressing jealousy). Each provides you with the correct amount of pain associated with the appropriate circumstance or event, for you personally. Your mind has programmed specific doses of pain before the event occurs, and then the actual event just triggers the release of that pain.

The dentist's office called recently, informing me of a cancellation. If I came right over I could get in immediately instead of waiting for my scheduled appointment several weeks later. I was in a serious quandary. I hate going to the dentist and part of me said, "But we haven't had sufficient time to worry about it yet," and another part of me said, "Just go get it over with *now!*" I hesitated and finally said, "What the heck, I'll come now." When I arrived I had no time to wait in the lobby reading, no paperwork, no idle chatting with the receptionist. I was ushered into the dental chair straightaway. As I sat there I realized I had not had time to connect with the Higher Self of the dentist and the hygienist, and had not prepared myself for the pain. I have sensitive teeth and it seems everything they do at the dentist's office hurts. Or so I thought.

As I sat there trying to find a quick connection with my guides, I heard this familiar voice say, "This *doesn't* have to feel like pain. If you label it as pain, it will feel like pain. Try labeling it as something else." I knew the voice to be my most trusted guide and it went on to say, "How would this be different from you being tortured as a prisoner?" I thought about that question and realized only that I was going to pay for this, that's the sole difference. "Why not rewire your response now, *in case* you get captured and tortured?" Strangely, the suggestion seemed reasonable to me.

My guide's voice went on to direct me with each prod of the metal instruments on my teeth. "Instead of labeling that feeling as pain, why not label it as *poking of the teeth*, which is very different from pain." I gave it a try. I was pretty nervous about this idea, however, and was prepared to suffer pain with the next *poking of the teeth*. I sat there trusting the best I could. So far, so good. The poking did not actually hurt. It simply felt like a poke and pokes, in general, don't really hurt. Next came the scraping of the teeth. Normally, that gets to me; I tense up and clasp my fingers together on my lap, fold my legs, and curl up my toes. But I was told to re-label the pain as *scraping of the teeth*. Ok, that did seem logical. Scraping is not really pain, it is something else. Then came the buffing, flossing, stuffing with dry cotton in preparation for X-rays and other innocuous things that embarrass me that I ever thought they were pain. By the time I left, I realized that this appointment was the very first dental experience of my life that did not include pain. I really think I had been given an opportunity to rewire a painful experience, turning it into something completely different, and I wasn't being prepared for torture after all.

Keep this idea in mind. What you *feel* is monitored, supervised and coordinated by the mind, *not* the body. Have you ever witnessed someone who has been hypnotized? You can tell them they are being burned by an ice cube and they will develop a burn blister. Conversely, you can tell them that burning coals are smooth river rocks, and they will cross them with no burns to their soles. The mind is doing the controlling, and while it may not be the conscious mind, it is not the body. If you believe something will heal you, you have a lot better chance of being healed. If you believe some medication prescribed to you is poison, it is unlikely that it will have healing effects. If you have heard and believe all kinds of rave reviews about a particular doctor or practitioner, you have conquered a good part of the ability to heal already. Your mind has set you up.

Let's take this idea a step further by determining how you can use this knowledge to reprogram sensations to be more desirable. You are the one who makes the rules, so you can change them. You want to move from an uncomfortable, outdated place to a more healed, whole and peaceful place. For example, if you feel like you are empty, without direction and lost, instead of calling the place Hell and referring to it as your home, re-label it, The Borderland. The word borderland indicates the presence of a border nearby. This process moves you from a negative thought of where you are and how it *feels*, to a place of infinite possibility. What does this border contain? How far is it? Are many borders nearby? Do you have choices? The imagination awakens and feeds you some of those possibilities. Your physical location has not changed, but you have allowed the mind and body to *feel* that something right around the corner contains your relief. Hell seems a lot more permanent when points of relief are not available. You transform your experience because you change the nature of it.

This discussion isn't just about taking something negative and turning it into something positive. I'm aware that negatively poled readers will be skeptical about that idea and scoff. I am merely suggesting that you re-label sensations when you reprogram the sensations you receive. This simply serves your journey better.

Let's say you are following this book's premise, making some serious changes in who you are, or rather who you *believe* you are. You have passed a lot of difficult tests, and you have let go of unwanted garbage from your past. It all led you to where you are right now. Even though your new mantra is about forgiveness, love and clarity, some things still push your buttons and you instantly feel anger and feelings of betrayal every time they happen. Truly, you want to grow and have your first response be the one that gets you *off* the hamster wheel instead of the one that locks you firmly into the repeated cycle. How do you do that? We have talked about some ideas, like consciously choosing other options and making choices about responding differently. The process is ideal *if* the mind operates before the emotions. Unfortunately, the emotions usually come and go and lay waste before the mind even knows what hit it. Remember, though, the mind was involved in the initial programming of that response in the first place.

Let's say you feel betrayed every time someone doesn't support you the way you think they should. This term, betrayal, comes with pain and hurt and keeps the door to forgiveness firmly shut. Yet, this is a problem if you want to grow in forgiveness, love and clarity. What do you do? If you have tried with your conscious brain to choose another response and you still receive the pain and hurt that comes with the experience of not being supported, then you simply must speak to the programmer. Locate the feeling of betrayal, acknowledge all the accompanying emotions, then pause. Say, "This experience of not being supported is now going to be labeled as 'not being supported'." That doesn't seem that difficult. I can think of a lot worse things than not being supported, like getting your *teeth poked*! Whatever emotions you may have for that experience, I imagine they are less intense than betrayal, which feels pretty harsh.

You subtract the pain and hurt from not being supported because you know that not being supported is what happens when others express differing points of view. One person may say, "I love you, but I can't support you because I simply disagree with your viewpoint." That's okay. They did not *betray* you, they simply exercised their right to express themselves in a free country. Now the process seems a lot easier. We can explore this concept of betrayal further. Let's say someone goes out on a date with someone other than you? You need to do some re-labeling. How about calling it 'when someone goes out with someone other than me'? This label feels a lot better than 'betrayal'. In the reprogramming, keep in mind your ideals of forgiveness, love, clarity, whatever they are and try to let the higher mind guide you. That means you can't include things like 'when someone treats me like a piece of trash'. You are looking to steer clear of blaming, but to accept responsibility in the re-labeling. The label reads quite differently as, 'when I allow myself to be treated like a piece of trash.' Read the other one again, 'when someone treats me like a piece of trash'. Which label feels like it has more control? Which one feels like someone else has the control? You are looking for growth and that includes responsibility.

You may remember your mom telling you at some young age that you were to be an example for other younger children and you could no longer indulge in childish antics or some such thing? We all must accept responsibility at some point along our spiritual journey, and depending upon our moms, our physical journey as well.

What about real pain, not just teeth poking and rough flossing, but the pain caused from internal hemorrhaging or cancer or strep throat? What difference does it make if we reprogram that kind of pain? We're going to either get better or die. So you may ask what would be the point of trying to re-label the pain as something else?

The point is serious and it is only for those on the spiritual path. A new label reinforces that *you are not your body*. If you die from some physical disease or ailment, you leave this life believing your body caused you to die, and that is not correct. Where will that leave you the next time, assuming there is a next time? It will leave you fearing the body's control and its ultimate death. Whenever you fear something, you know what happens; you draw it to you like static electricity to a balloon on shag carpeting.

The concept of re-labeling or reprogramming goes far beyond the immediate pain you may be feeling. It is rewiring you into a bionic being. Think about those people you know with a high pain tolerance. They are capable of doing things long after the rest of us would have stopped, and whether or not they have repercussions later is also programming. What if you believed you were the master of your body, which you are? You would be able to heal yourself, which you already do, but you would be able to do it consciously. It's like the idea of the body as a vehicle again. If you had a vehicle that sometimes stalled in the most inopportune places and important automotive parts fell off just when you needed them the most, you wouldn't trust this vehicle much. You might stay home more or you might just start out every adventure with mixed emotions of excitement and fear. On the other hand, what if you had a vehicle that always started every single time you turned the key, and never let you down or had to go to the shop, or even sputtered, you would begin each travel adventure with great enthusiasm.

Though the idea of re-labeling goes against traditional thoughts about the physical body, I am asking you to try it. If you look to the *mind* for every pain the body could ever have, from teensy weensy to giant size, you are going to the source, you are taking control, you are rewiring the master circuit breaker. If you relabeled *hunger* as *boredom*, as it is in most cases, imagine how the message would translate to the body. You would not look to food to fill a need such as boredom, and consequently, you would not detest the body for growing fat. You could redirect the activities of the mind to accommodate for boredom.

People who have been stabbed with a knife say that they are surprised that the pain does not actually feel *stabbing* as they suspected; instead they report a dull and all encompassing feeling. If this phenomenon is true maybe the pains you are labeling are preprogrammed responses and are not really what the sensations actually feel like. Perhaps they can be described or re-labeled in other ways that are less restricting, more inspiring, or more powerful, as with Hell versus Borderland. Which concepts provide infinite possibilities, because that is what the universe is, and which ones leave you stuck in your comfortable past?

Can Sensations be Misinterpreted?

Have you ever shut your eyes in the city and listened to the distant sound of cars on the highway? What does it sound like? Cars on a highway? Have you ever closed your eyes and listened to a rushing river or creek in a forest and imagined it sounded just like a busy highway in the city or that the cars sounded like a rushing river? They all sound uncommonly similar; only the smells and your labeling differentiate them.

I remember long ago sitting on the back of a motorcycle while my boyfriend filled the tank with gas. I was sitting in a daze, staring at something, dreamy, not paying any attention when I got a strong whiff of the gasoline. I thought, what is that? It smells delightful and it tingles my nose. I breathed it in, not thinking what it was, but I was enjoying it. Then my boyfriend woke me out of my reverie to apologize for the really stinky gasoline fumes, and he wondered how I could stand the smell. In a moment of realization, I recalibrated my smell sensors to not enjoy the smell of gasoline knowing they were toxic, but I still have the feeling of that strangely delightful experience.

Have you ever heard a noise, like a vine scraping against a window in the wind, that sounds so much like a baby crying that your body actually has the physiological stimulation of rescue before you can figure out what it really is? What about the sound of a pack of coyotes and a group of wild teenagers? Strangely, one experience feels like you are privy to a special moment in nature, whereas the other feels like you are unfortunate in your juxtaposition to partying teens. They sound exactly alike, and only our interpretation is different. So many times in our lives, if we pay attention to them, our sensations are misinterpreted. It is not a bad thing; it is evidence that our sensations may have multiple interpretations. If you accept that premise, you might try to become actively involved in that reprogramming or reinterpretation.

Years ago I lived in a neighborhood that was also home to a family of skunks. My predisposition at the time was to smell skunks and feel sick. I thought that skunks smelled horrid. When I asked the lady who lived downstairs how she could stand the smell, she said she not only didn't mind the skunks, but they made her think of earthy things. She actually enjoyed them. At the time, I thought she was mis-wired. In reality, she was just wired differently than I was. So if sensations can be misinterpreted, or interpreted any way you like, then they can be reprogrammed as well.

Let's look at pain again. This is the greatest impetus, I think, to want to try this sensation reprogramming. I work with a healing practitioner who employs trigger point therapy as a pain release technique in his sessions. I have been in his office often and heard various responses to his work. Some grown men, who seem very manly, will cry out in pain and attempt to hit the doctor, whereas others leave the office feeling like they just had a rejuvenating massage. One day I chatted with a patient who was leaving, and he said the treatment was so calming it could easily put him to sleep. Other people I have queried say that if it weren't so painful they might come back. Some even call the doctor, Doctor Pain. Why the difference? Do we all just have different pain receptors, some of us missing a few, some with too many? Or do we all have different concepts of pain? Do some of us enlist extra nerve receptors when we feel pain is imminent?

How do you take back control from the body and return it to the mind? How do you understand that the body is a vehicle for communication and expression while you are in a manifest experience? Who programmed the body in the first place, and is it on autopilot? How do you live a more peaceful, healthy and whole life? Do you have to get old, decay, hurt more and eventually die?

The bottom line is this. You need to really understand, not just conceptualize with the brain, that you are not this lovely body you call *me*. You are something more, something that is not trapped in a physical body, but that is always free. You are capable of knowing your spirit or the Mind of God, or whatever you want to call it, and as you do you will know for certain that you cannot ever die. Your vehicle may need to be traded in or sold or discarded, but *you,* the you that you now know, cannot be hurt or poisoned or murdered or anything at all. When you remove that ultimate fear, you remove all the fear-laden indicators (like pain) that waylay your journey.

Reprogram to Build Self-Esteem

After you have reprogrammed sensations that trigger unpleasant or limiting responses, try using the same technique to help build self-esteem. To intimately know who you truly are, repairing self-esteem is essential.

For example, one issue that just about every woman struggles with is her weight. I want you to assess the feelings you have about the various parts of your body right now. Start with your head and go down. How do you feel about the shape of your skull, your hair, your face, your lips, your eyes, your neck? Now what are the feelings that come up for you as you encounter your shoulders, your upper arms, your fingers, your breasts? Now watch as you get to your tummy. What feelings arise? Watch too as you encounter your derriere and hips. We are getting into unwelcome territory. Stomach, hips, thighs…they carry some energy that creates feelings in your body when you touch or look at them. Sometimes even sitting at your desk you are plagued by how uncomfortable these body parts feel just sitting there. Continue on down to your legs, knees, ankles, feet, and toes. You have pre-programmed all your feelings about them, so you must reprogram them before you can lose weight.

Think of it like this (the thinking is what is doing the programming). You wear a certain size, perhaps bigger than you want to admit, but it is your current size. Your pants fit around your stomach but they are tight so they won't fall off. What if you wore a size 6 or a size 2? Wouldn't you wear your pants with about the same tightness? Wouldn't they feel exactly the same? Your stomach would feel constrained when you bent over or sat down no matter what size pants you wear. So that feeling of tightness around your stomach should not be labeled 'fat', it should be labeled 'waistband' feeling. How does the ego want you to interpret waistband? It wants you to feel dissatisfied so 'fat' would be the perfect label. But, happily, we are no longer engaging in the ego's games, so 'waistband' it is. You not only re-label the feeling, but you rename your body parts.

Years ago a client of mine, a gorgeous blonde, mentioned that she was having trouble looking in the mirror nude. I asked her why, because from what I could see, if she was having trouble, the rest of the women in the world should break all their mirrors! She didn't know. I suggested that she stand in front of the mirror naked and start from the top and go down, assessing her feelings about each body part. She reported later that she did this. She said she was perfectly contented until she got to her female organs. The whole region around her vagina and uterus made her want to turn away. She said that having contracted herpes from an unfaithful husband made her feel ashamed and betrayed. She was amazingly aware, stepping right into the origination of those feelings. I then suggested that she make friends with this alienated body area. She needed to do something that pampered and felt joyful to her female self and then rename the body area. It was important that she remove all history from it, or whatever creative thing she could imagine to incorporate this part of her into the rest of the working force vehicle. She said that it wasn't easy to do. She always wanted to turn away and never look right at it. She finally got a mirror out and examined it in detail, she bought some lovely lotions and powders, and after consciously bringing the energy of her vagina and uterus back into line with the rest of her body, she was happy to report that she could look from head to toe stark naked and feel renewed. However, it was not without some self-examination of feelings she had stored about her responses to her ex-husband's affair and his unwillingness to admit or discuss it. This body part had been storing those emotions, and so each time she looked at it, it reminded her of something she didn't want to think about. Bringing it into awareness, examining it in detail, re-labeling it, learning from it, not hiding it away, and taking responsibility for participating in its redirection, were all part of the transformation.

If you look at the overweight body again, can you take this reprogramming a step further and begin to change the way you feel about your body? Your mind has done all the programming. Why not allow or consciously choose to reprogram what you need to build self-esteem, not just release you from pain? Can you program a sensation of feeling thin above any self-criticism that pops up when you think of yourself as fat? Are there parts of you that are bigger than others? Try to see what they are doing there energetically. They may be protecting you from something or someone. You may have worries or traumas stored there. Are you ready to let them out and then change the labels they carry? Can you monitor the thoughts you have about your body and notice when you have negative ones? Maybe you have just been visiting your mother or grandmother and feel a biological pull to their weight, which drains your energy and depresses your feelings about yourself. Or maybe you are being called grandmother or grandfather for the first time, triggering programs you have about what grandparents look and feel like. Have you been hanging out with someone anorexic or very thin, over-dramatizing the size of your healthy body?

Be aware, take control back from errant egoic thinking, and be creative about how and when to reprogram sensations. Doing so is a major step, in not only building self-esteem, but in turning more power over to the spirit mind.

"Intuition is a spiritual faculty and does not explain, but simply points the way."

— Florence Scovel Shinn

11 Guidance and Trust

One skill that needs reinforcing and encouraging is listening to your own wisdom. No matter how often I suggest to others that they have guidance available to them through their own highest wisdom, people still think I have something they do not have. No one is special in that regard. We all have equal access. In qualifying the specifics one more time, I'll attempt to drive home the concept that decisions and responses can be made *with* greater wisdom instead of trial and error. You need a voice of guidance from outside the illusion to find truth. Wouldn't it be nice just to have some help, some concern about your actual, specific problem even though you know it isn't the biggest thing in the world? Hearing and following guidance can make the difference between repeating the same melodrama of your life play and stepping into a realm where the script includes free-flowing joy!

Why Can't I Hear My Guidance?

The most common question I hear in my line of work is, "Why can't I hear my guidance?" I have struggled with all sorts of possible answers. Then one day, exhausted from trying to inspire, and feeling like I had failed to completely answer that question, I asked my own guidance why some people believe they cannot hear their own guidance. The response came as the following.

First of all, what is guidance? It is a form of organic wisdom that inspires, directs, or affirms and it is organized in a way that has meaning to the one perceiving it. It is not necessarily a voice, as you may expect it to be. It can be a host of things, ranging from billboards or license plates, to knowings that come from an epiphany, intuition or voices in your head. It may come though music on hold while you're awaiting a response to your call, quotes in a book you flip though, scenes in a movie or book, repeated themes or numbers, feelings, tears, hairs standing up on the back of your neck, or goose bumps. It can be odd things at specific times: two people saying the exact same thing at the exact same moment, a joke, a poem, something symbolic, or a dream. It can be a message from a loved one who has passed on, it can be an arm that appears to come out of thin air at just the right moment to steer a car away from disaster, it can be a jolt of awareness at an uncanny moment to prevent a tragic event. It can be a sense of déjà vu, reminding, guiding, directing, alerting, whatever needs to happen to bring special awareness to a particular situation. And it can be a sense of intuitively knowing which way to go, which brand to choose, what to avoid, and when to avoid it for some seemingly unknown reason.

All that being said, it would seem almost impossible what you have not had at least *one* of those experiences of guidance. Yet while most people do receive guidance in bizarre moments and are grateful, they would like to access that wisdom for everyday problems and comfort, not just in unpredictable moments of crisis.

Secondly, it is important to keep in mind that everyone interprets the world in a different way. Some people are verbal, some are feeling, others are practical and still others are emotional or dramatic. Each person is going to receive their guidance in a different way, even different ways on different days, depending upon the seeker. So in looking for a daily routine of asking questions and accepting guidance you must look for the method that suits you best. It would be convenient if you could choose the process, but it doesn't seem to be the case. Most people I work with would like the answers to come in black and white on printed stationery, with their name clearly legible in their mother tongue, folded and neatly tucked into the pillowcase every morning. So far, I haven't seen this to be the predominant method of receiving guidance.

I once spoke with a woman about this question and suggested that she may have received guidance, but didn't recognize it as such. She assured me that she had not received any guidance from divine sources in any way. Then, I enumerated the many ways she might prepare herself, by opening up and narrowing down her questions. Finally, after my many illustrations of ways guidance comes through, she said, "Well, I *do* write to God, and I *feel* the answer." For crying out loud! That's guidance, pure and simple. She thought it was just her own heart doing unexplainable things after she wrote her innermost grievances to God. Let me say, that is guidance, okay?

Guidance will use whatever tools it finds or thinks you might clue in on to assist, inspire or direct you. Depending upon how creative you are, or how open you are to reading the world around you in a different and even personal way, you may find elaborate and even funny methods as well.

One woman I know says she was driving away from a hospital after leaving her husband in Intensive Care, feeling overwhelming anguish and sorrow. As she drove, she was thinking, "I cannot do this, I cannot manage our life without you, raise our children, live through your debilitating disease. I cannot." Just then she looked up to see Winston Churchill on a billboard saying, "Never, never give up." In that one instant, she felt not only that the message was meant for her specifically, but that she could and would find the will to manage.

Another woman, obviously more creative than most, was leaving a movie theatre crying from the emotional drama of the movie, feeling quite alone and unloved. Long ago, she had prenamed a man, William, whom she knew to be her (as yet unmet in this lifetime) soul mate. As she was leaving the theatre, she felt his absence deep in her soul. She glanced over to a car in the parking lot with a license plate of WLU55. Her birthday was May 5th, and she interpreted the license plate to be saying, "William Loves U, May 5th!!" In one brief glance, she was fulfilled, knowing that even though she had yet to meet this soul mate in this incarnation, he was providing messages of love for her until they reunited.

How Can I Hear My Own Guidance?

Whatever way you receive your messages from guidance, you need to become acquainted with it. That is your job. You must make a space for messages to be received. It's just like wanting to get music from the radio; first you must connect the radio to some power source, turn it on and tune it to the right station. In the case of receiving messages from guidance, *you* become the radio. So the first thing you need to do is *plug yourself into a power source*. In other words, reroute some of your vital, living energy to this task. You cannot be doing the laundry, watching television and babysitting and still have power left for a serious session of guidance. You need to stop other activities, place yourself in a quiet, undisturbed space, bring your attention (energy) to the act of asking for/receiving guidance and allow your breathing to be clear and long. Automatically, you will find yourself in a calmer place. Now you have brought power to the radio.

Next you must turn on the radio. *State your intention*. You want to speak to your higher council, your guides, celestial teachers, helpers, spiritual assistance, angels, Jesus, God, whatever you choose, based on your belief system. When you turn on and set your intention, make sure you ask for those guides that resonate with the highest vibration of the Divine. This way you are receiving the highest counsel. The guidance you are asking for ultimately comes from your *own* highest self; you just don't recognize it as such yet. But as you come to know more fully who you are, you will know you are the one who contains this divine counsel. However, until such time, or knowing, it is empowering and helpful to imagine separate guides or angels assisting you. Even the voice of Christ will eventually become your own voice when you realize, or when he tells you, that you are One and the Same. Later we will discuss this further.

Next, *you tune in.* As with radio frequencies, whether or not you are tuning in, the airwaves are still out there with the messages of that station. That's how it is with metaphysical messages also. They are always there, available to any of us at any time, but it is up to us to tune in. I used to think I had to maintain a vibration of a very high nature to be able to hear, but this is not the case. You simply have to become familiar with what frequency to seek. When you are in a calm and joy-filled place, your vibration is higher and easier to locate, but it is not necessary. How often do you ask for guidance in a joyful and light attitude? Most of the time you are looking for assistance because something is wrong or at least worrisome. It isn't always that easy to maintain a higher state. Once again, you must become familiar with the location of the vibration. The only way I know how to do that is by practicing, trying again and again. It's like that with sports or music or any number of things; you struggle with the correct hand position, body posture or level of strength to apply until you get it. A teacher may explain it a hundred different ways, but until you actually understand what your piano teacher means when she says, "touching the keys like a kitten is pawing them," then it is all just words.

Imagine a river of wisdom flowing through your room. Yes, somewhere invisible in your meditation room is a river, endlessly flowing with abundant resources, information, inspiration and wisdom. All you have to do is locate it and dive in. It is always flowing for anyone to access. I don't say this for you to feel bad if you can't access it, but only for you to know that it really exists. Just experiment with tuning in and then, remember, your own way of hearing will be your own. You may have a feeling that fills your heart or stomach, you may hear a voice (maybe your own voice), you may sense that you know something you didn't know before, or maybe a grand solution will just pop into your head.

Do you know the story about the little child who prayed to God every night for a bicycle? When the child finally received a bright blue bicycle from Santa for Christmas, he then prayed to God, "Thanks anyway, I already got one." It is like that with guidance. Many times I have asked my guidance if a splendid idea that came to my mind was, in fact, suitable for the solution, only to be queried, "Exactly *where* did you think that idea came from *anyway?*"

Tuning in may be problematical for most people and cause them to give up way too soon. You are always a receiver of energy. You pick up on other people's emotions all the time. You hear things that aren't being said, intonations that betray emotions other than those being expressed. You see eye movements and avoidances at strange moments. All those things express emotions that words don't convey. If you look at your day and observe how often you receive and send off energy, you will see that it's really not that hard to tune in to a celestial frequency transmitting divine guidance. After all, it is worth the effort too. The payoff is eternal, truly.

Imagine a bank of energy. You are sitting centered and open in your quiet place and in front of is a short wall of energy. It is easy to access. Then imagine your mind going higher than that, over that wall to a second wall of energy. This wall is another layer and a little harder to access; but once your mind has detected how to locate it, you can return to it at will. Now imagine a third wall of energy, higher than the others and finer in vibration. Each layer is a wave or wall of energy, and each is finer in vibration or higher in wisdom than the others. Proceed a little higher till you bump into it. And you will. If you do not have the patience to pause at each one, go right to the higher wall if you can find it. But either way, the proof of your finding it is in the messages and guidance you receive.

How to Ask?

I suggest beginning your inquiry with questions that have a yes or no answer. This way you can narrow your possibilities of reply to two or perhaps three choices. For example, if you want to know about possibilities for your future, don't ask an open-ended questions like, "What do you think?" You will most likely hear nothing. What do you think about what? About your future? About the relationships in your future, about your spirituality in the future, about your career, etc? Narrow the question to, "Would this be in my highest interest to do this?" (yes/no) "Or should I do this?" (yes/no) You may be steered in a direction, but if you don't pick up anything subtle or anything at all, the answer is probably neither one. You then ask about departments. Categorize things into departments such as work life, home life, family, social life, etc. If you have ways of dividing issues, like with the chakras, houses of the zodiac, numerology, traditional psychology, seasons, then offer to use any of those means to narrow the issues. However creative you can be, they will work with you. Then when you get to that department, for example, the 4th Chakra, does it now have to do with intimate relationships, issues of betrayal, issues of worth, being able to be loved, being able to honor the self? If you have framed it regarding a career, does it concern doing something with others, relationship counseling, something you love, or something that involves connecting with others?

Be creative in finding ways to simplify your list of optional choices, at least in the beginning. After you find a clear channel repeatedly, you can carry on lengthy open-ended conversations as often as you have the energy for it.

Steer clear from questions like, "Is this the best choice?" What is best to an enlightened counselor? What is best for your spiritual journey, your mother's health, your community standing? *You need to clarify and be specific if you are looking for a specific answer.* If you feel you have tuned into the right channel but can't hear anything, either rephrase your question or turn things off. If you are tired or so overwhelmed with anxiety that you cannot find a clear channel, don't frustrate yourself. Come back another time. If you are constantly bumping into the same wall, and not receiving anything helpful, maybe that in itself is an answer. It may be saying you are not open or neutral, and are so fixated on hearing a certain result that you are not open for any other possibility.

That's another thing, *you need to be neutral.* If you are already sure you want a certain outcome, you are not open to receiving true guidance, you just want a divine confirmation. Before you ask the question, imagine receiving an answer contrary to what you personally desire. If you feel disappointed or mad, then you are not neutral. Sit quietly, allow yourself to see the situation from another perspective or even from a distant time. Sit there until you hear the contrary answer and it feels the same as the one you had previously desired. It doesn't mean that your guidance will always tell you things you don't want to hear. It's quite the contrary. You just need to be open enough to be able to hear something you may not even *expect*. Often I am told that my mind does not contain the answer and that I have not allowed myself to imagine boldly enough. I just have to come back later and play charades or whatever I can think of that might enlighten me.

What if you are stubborn? What if you think that you are so cursed or doomed or neglected that no one will ever speak to you? Then I suggest that you may receive your guidance in other ways, and you *will* receive it, everyone does whether they want to believe it or not. You may have an active dream life, with plenty of symbolism to unravel your worst fears and enough material to face your greatest challenges. You may receive wisdom from unexpected sources like billboards, or movie dialogues or whatever you avail yourself to—even pop-ups on the Internet. It is common also to receive your answer at a later, random time, after you have long forgotten you even asked. Sometimes we are not ready to receive the answer at the time we ask, even though we think we are, because we may not have let go of some fear or preconception that is preventing the genuine guidance from being received.

One especially stubborn man asked me many times about his failure to find any guidance, though he had asked over a million times (he swore he counted them all). I convinced him to give me the whole story, what he did, how often, how much effort, etc. He certainly seemed to be earnest in his attempts. I then asked about his method of receiving guidance, and it seems he was expecting a thundering voice of the Old Testament God while he was speaking to Moses (as dramatized by Cecil B. DeMille's movie, *The Ten Commandments*). I knew this man was a gentle and emotional type, feeling was his main source of information, so I suspected a need to look elsewhere for his answers. He was really struggling with depression and could not seem to find his way out of it. Finally, after making an inquiry into every possible guidance vehicle I could think of, I asked about his dreams. He readily admitted he believed dreams were simply mental garbage, but I learned that he had been having abnormally terrible dreams about his wife. Even though he loved her dearly, almost every night his dreams took him into a situation with her where he was yelling at her, sometimes kicking her or berating her. She never behaved correctly, and he was always trying to take control. Then finally, he dreamed that she was getting a rope to hang herself, and he yelled that he knew she wouldn't do such a thing. But she did. She took the rope, tied it to a lamp hanging from the ceiling and hung herself. She didn't appear to die from the hanging and he yanked her off the lamp and proceeded to beat and kick her for just thinking of killing herself.

Subscribing to Freud's dream theory that every player in the dream is an aspect of the dreamer, I was shocked at the violent nature of these dreams. I asked if he had pent-up aggressions towards his wife, and he said nowhere in his conscious mind. I then asked him to sum up in one concept what his wife represented to him. He did not have any idea, he said, and wanted me to just figure it out or ask my guidance for him. However, this message was personal. It was for him and it was important that he figure it out. I asked him to imagine sitting in a bar years after his wife had died, explaining to someone next to him what his wife was to him, what she represented. Just then his eyes filled with tears and he said, "Joy, simply joy." With those words, he had unraveled the dream mystery. He was trying to destroy, berate, and eliminate any spontaneity of his *own* joy. That was a serious message trying to get through, but the depression was too thick a barrier to allow any other means to penetrate. It may have been the first step in recognizing the sabotage relating to his depression. Maybe until he decides to let his mind open to the possibilities that he deserves divine guidance in a simpler form, his dreams will be a valid vehicle for his wisdom.

One of my clients shared with me a great story of creative guidance. We had just finished a session together and he was traveling by car to his work, in traffic. He was thinking of all the things our session brought up for him, and specifically about the woman he was presently estranged from, but for whom he had deep feelings. He was tossing it over in his mind about calling her. He knew that some of the issues that came up for him in our session would allow him to have a stronger, more connected relationship, even though he had not communicated with her in almost 3 months and had promised he would not contact her until at least 3 months had passed. He wanted to uphold his promise, yet at the same time, felt that the time was right to reconnect. His commitment to her was stronger than ever. All these thoughts were bouncing around in his head when he looked up and saw a billboard advertising a exotic sports car. It read, "She wants you as much as you want her." He grabbed his cell phone and called her immediately. He confessed to me later that they ended up talking that night for 7 hours. I guess she did want him after all.

The more prone you are to being independent and doing it all yourself, the more creative your guides will have to be. If you believe you have assistance from outside yourself, or from your own highest self, or however you come to think of it, then you will be more apt to receive guidance more effortlessly. The more you ask, the more you will be prone to ask, and the more guidance you receive. This truth always comes home to me when wise counsel from my divine guides solves something I have been fretting over. For example, if I allow them to assist me with *one* thing, why am I so stubbornly holding on to the idea that I have to figure out my *other* harder problems myself? Is there any problem too hard for God that I could figure it out better or sooner? When I think about it, I realize I am holding out on even other problems. Think about it like this: in all of human history—past, present and future—is your problem really that unique? It may feel like it, but I assure you, guidance has seen it before.

As we're all connected, sometimes you will be the messenger for someone else and sometimes they will be one for you. Every week for over 6 years I have written an inspirational quotation on the white board at my husband's clinic so his patients can see it as they enter the office. I ask for guidance when choosing the quotation. After many years, every single week at least one patient, and sometimes it's the mail or delivery person, says, "That quote was *exactly* what I needed to hear" or, "I know that is for me this week, isn't it?" They think I have inside information about the metaphysical nature of all the people who enter the office. I assure them it *is* for them, because it is.

Asking About the Future

One department needs discussion all by itself and that is asking about the future. First of all, what is the future? Traditionally speaking, you think of the future as the present you just haven't gotten to yet, but your guides operate in a different sphere of time or, rather, timelessness.

Let's imagine time in a different way. Imagine for a moment that the future thing you are asking about has already happened. If that were the case, it would be simple to determine the answer, right? You just pull up the records, access, and voila! But the human mind says, "Wait a minute, how can it be that easy, it hasn't happened yet. It must be harder than that, there must be some variable of change or some theory that says it cannot be known for certain." What I want to suggest is spherical time as opposed to linear time where Tuesday comes after Monday, which follows Sunday, and so on through eternity. In spherical time, everything is happening all at once. The way I like to explain it to non-physics students is using an example of dust in the windowsill. Imagine blowing on the dust in your windowsill in the sunlight. You see thousands of little dust particles all over the place magnified by the sunlight? Now think of each of those dust particles as a time bubble, or a moment of time containing an experience or a feeling or nothing meaningful; it's just a time bubble. That is what spherical time is like. You can see all at once that the life you may have had in 1792 is right there by the childhood traumas of 1968 or by the now of the present year. The events of 2045 are swirling right next to 1066. The year 1945 is happening right next to 3245 and 2097 BC is happening just as clearly as 2097 AD. This is a difficult concept for the human mind to grasp, some believe our minds are not equipped for it, but let's use it as an expansive concept right now.

Now, if spherical time exists, and is truer than is linear time in the universal picture, it is quite possible that we *and* our guides have access to any time bubble anywhere. What I am suggesting is that even though you may still not believe you can foretell the future, when you approach your guidance with a question about tomorrow, you can be a lot more open if you entertain the idea of spherical time. I believe that many people are so fixed in their thought process about what is *difficult* and what is *impossible*, that they essentially block their own guidance. If you believed what you were asking was easy to ascertain, you would not only expect the answer, you might have to remind yourself to have gratitude. For example, when a client is running late for a phone session, I quietly ask my guidance if the client is on the way to the phone, or if they need to be reminded that I am awaiting their call. I receive an affirmation or negative response right away. Then I relax and shortly the phone rings. However, if I ask if someone is going to call me tomorrow at a certain time, I don't feel so confident about the answer. Why? It's because I have a mental block about future events being impossible to foretell, even though the question about the client calling me in 5 minutes is a future event too! I tend to think of the next 5 minutes as part of *now*. But unless it's happening in this moment, it is not part of the human construct known as now.

We limit our ability to *hear* answers because we think we are accessing what we don't believe is possible to access. Ambiguous things associated with the future are easier, because there's no ability to confirm or deny. But questions associated with the more tangible future carry a dubitable energy. We tend not to believe the answers.

Also, the way you word the questions and the sense of neutrality or, rather non-neutrality, may set you up for failure or disappointment. Just as you would ask someone for something, knowing they will say no, you hedge your bet. You set your question up to sound like you weren't expecting it anyway. Then the one doing the giving doesn't feel obligated or even that you really want it. I am not suggesting that your guides judge you according to the way you ask a question; I am alluding to the vibration again. Access to guidance is neutral. Anyone can access it; you simply have to be on the right frequency, and self-effacement is not the right station. Ask your questions, knowing full well that you have every right to receive the answers; they come as part of your birthright. Choose to hear the answers as opposed to begging for some desperately needed help.

There are many frequencies on which we can hear our guidance, and genuine desire is one way to tune into the right ones for us. Sometimes I sit perfectly upon my zafuton cushion like a lovely Buddhist asking for divine guidance, and I hear nothing but the ringing in my ears. Other times I am so upset and mad that I demand a response, and I mean it, and I get it. Most of the time, asking for guidance is going to be part of your daily ritual, like getting dressed or eating breakfast. The emotional flavor to retain is honest, and passionate inquiry. On the days I have no questions, and some days I don't, I ask if my guidance has something to say to *me*. They respond as if they had been trying to get the floor for weeks, but my mind had been dancing all over it! Then they give me some information that changes the way I proceed or urges me to consider something I hadn't thought about in regard to what I am doing.

Your guidance will be more creative in making itself known to you when you have genuine desire to know, to grow, to have, and to become. Never, ever give up.

SECTION THREE
RECOGNIZING REALITY

"Essentially, all healing is the release from fear." – A Course in Miracles

12 Fear and Love

Walking the Cat Back: Turn Negative Thoughts into Joy

The questions arise, "What do I do on a minute-by-minute basis to change my world? How do I stop having negative thoughts? How do I begin to have joy?"

There is a spy term that applies to the process of digging out a mole in an operation called *walking the cat back*. We're going to apply it to rooting out the mole in our thought system.

I agree that it is very difficult to simply say, "I want to feel happy even though I don't, and I don't see any reason to feel happy." My suggestion is not to shift the *feelings* until you have shifted the mind. Since the mind holds the key to the feelings, let's start with thoughts. Consider an average day filled with average thoughts. Some of those thoughts are fine, some are filled with anxiety, some are pleasant and some are negative. Life seems to go like that, good days and bad ones. But the idea is, why tolerate the bad ones if this is indeed your own illusion?

Start with a thought. It might be the one you are dwelling on in the background right now. Perhaps it's one that has been moderately nagging you for some time. Instead of avoiding the thought, or distracting yourself to forget about it, or even pretending it isn't there, turn all of your attention to it for a moment.

For example, Frannie, who is fretting over her business, may think, "I am really, really nervous about that money I have to come up with to cover the expenses of moving my business. It is way too much anyway, and I can't believe I agreed to it now that I think about it. I feel like I'm in a bind because it is going to strap the company and we may not recover for many months." That series of thoughts will spawn sister or children thoughts that sound like: "Perhaps I have been taken for a ride in this whole move thing. I should never have listened to Bill and should have gotten more quotes." or, "What was wrong with the old building? We could have just let a few people go, rearranged the offices and made do. Sally hasn't been doing a good day's work anyway, why do I even keep her on? Geez, I really feel like the fool, being everyone's sugar daddy. Well, I've had enough of it. It's my company and I'm paying all this out just to accommodate some pretty pathetic losers." Depending upon the time of night that the first thought occurred, this thought process could go on and on and send her out into a perfect state of anxiety by the time the alarm goes off in the morning.

Now let's walk the cat back. Let's look at the fear behind the whole string of thoughts. Back off of the resentment towards Sally because that is superficial. Is Frannie really having anxiety that Sally isn't doing a good day's job? No, in fact, she is a fine worker. Back through those thoughts. Does she really feel she has been taken advantage of? No, Bill has been a good friend for years and she knows he has given her as good a deal as anyone. Could she really continue to stay in the old building and allow her business to expand? No, she has known for 2 years this moment was inevitable. So, what comes next? Is she worried that the company won't recover? Well, actually sales have been up and if she figures correctly, her estimation is that it will be transparent in 3 months. Then what is waking her up at 3:00 am?

Is it the fear that she will go broke? Back that thought upstream. She is wading into fear waters. Is she afraid that she cannot make decisions that are always in the best interest of all her employees? Is she afraid that someone or everyone will be mad or upset with her if she does or doesn't do something different? Suddenly she is hitting survival issues, and they will usually be somewhere in the realm of fear. The anxiety is coming from the ultimate fear of doing something irreversible that will make everyone remove their love and admiration from her and will leave her broke and homeless. Maybe that is the last thing Frannie uncovers at about 4:30 am.

At this point she must hold on to this primal fear thought and kindly say, "Do you *really* think we are going to end up under a bridge with nothing to eat and no one to love us?" Probably not, however, just like consoling a child who sees a monster in the jacket slung over a chair in the dark, kindness and reassurance are helpful at this point. Imagine you are Frannie and think of the people in your life who really would take you in if, in fact, you lost everything and were homeless. And even if you can't think of anyone, or your fear convinces you that these people will turn on you too, then remind yourself of this final truth. Even if you really *do* end up under a bridge and starve to death, the ultimate lack of personal survival, *death will not change who you truly are one iota.* The body is only a temporary house for a material experience and how you were created is immutable, it can never be changed. In consolation, speak these words with confidence and finality. Remind yourself that this fear is only that, a fear. But it is no longer hidden, and recognizing it is the same as turning on the light. "Look, honey, it is just your jacket here on the chair. Look, Frannie, you are more dearly loved than you know, you will not starve to death." The light dispels the fear created by the rampant thoughts of a human being living in a world of many potential fears.

Dispelling fear is just what you are doing. You are turning the light on the fear. You are saying, "Is *this* what I am afraid of?" Then you realize that it isn't that bad, that it's really not the end of the world after all. It may feel like the end of the world, but it is never the end of your immortal self. The basis for much fear is that we will ultimately die from a decision or action. Remember, you will find either fear or love at the base camp of any thought process, so hiking back down to find who is in charge is all that is required to shift a mood or worry. If love is present, worry is absent, so you simply need to reassign control from a fear-based partnership to that of love.

Once you have walked the cat back, turned on the light, seen the helpless jacket lying innocently on the chair, you will find that sleep will come with no effort at all. Or if you are awake and truly want to choose joy, now that the thoughts generated from fear are gone, replace them with ones that generate love, happiness, contentment, joy or peace. How do you do that? Start with an overlay of something you desire. Something or someone that brings you joy, makes you laugh, starts you giggling or brings a sense of peace. For example, if you love riding your motorcycle in the desert and watching the sun set, then remember the last time you did that with someone you loved. If you love fishing and it brings you peace, call up a memory of a time when you were fishing and it felt particularly peaceful. Or imagine a place you'd like to go.

My niece is an officer in NOAA (National Oceanic and Atmospheric Administration) and toured a few family members around her ship. I was impressed simply that she could dock such a huge beast. I knew what it was like captaining even a small sailboat. The tour encompassed many floors that all looked alike and I couldn't really find anything to relate to when we came to a series of cartoons pasted on the door of their cafeteria. She stopped us and made us read them, expecting us all to laugh as hard as she had when they had been posted. However, they were all relating to the work they do at NOAA and no one laughed. She asked me if I didn't find them funny, because I am usually the first to giggle at anything. I said, in fact, I found them hysterical, but was saving the laughter for another time when I needed it more. We got a laugh out of that, but the conversation continued over dinner. I explained that it was a tactic for being more in charge of your own moods or happiness. Sometimes when you don't have anything to laugh about, or any reason to be joyful, look into your can of collected treasures and pull one out. Turn it over in your mind and revel in its every facet. Pretty soon, placing yourself in that space energetically, you will be back there and will have changed the vibration of your mood. Your feelings will accommodate and you will have changed the direction of your day. She assured me it would come in really handy after they had been at sea for months in northern Alaska!

The brutal fact is this: no one can make you fall asleep and no one can face your fears. You have to learn to do both. When you don't master the first, you know how unpleasant life can be. When you don't master the second, those fears will plague you forever and ever, life after endless life, until you do. The effort required to walk the cat back a time or two or even a hundred if that's what you need, will net such positive results you will start to do it effortlessly again and again; however, mustering the energy to do it once can seem horrendous.

One of my clients suggested to her teenage daughter, Lucy, that when she was having a particularly bad day and felt out of control, angry or frustrated, that she should write in a notebook each and every thing that she was upset about. Then when she was finished, they could address each of them and see whether or not they could do anything about them. The next time Lucy came home ranting and raving at her mother, the notebook was produced and was handed quickly to the out-of-control teen.

About 15 minutes later, the anger had subsided and she had exhausted her list of worries. They read each of them together. The first worry was that she didn't believe her mother loved her or wanted to talk to her. She said she really just needed a hug. Lucy's mother stopped reading and pulled her daughter close and hugged her tightly. Her daughter started crying and sobbing, releasing all the negative energy she had pent up all day. Finally they resumed reading the list, and the remaining items really didn't look that bad. For instance, she had written that her best friend was a bitch. She admitted now that she wasn't really a bitch. She had done this one thing but now Lucy was willing to forgive and forget. It didn't seem to be that big of a deal now. She had also written that she thought she had failed a test in school. Knowing what kind of student she was, her mother asked, "Do you really think you failed it?" Lucy admitted she probably hadn't failed it, and the next day brought the test home with a score of 92 out of 100, a far cry from failing. Lucy's fear that day was simply that she was alone with the weight of the world, separated from the love she so desired, without anyone to help her or love her.

Try this tactic, or a variation of it, on yourself. If you need to make a similar list, make a place to do that. If you need to innumerate the issues, then do so. If you need to talk out loud to your fear, or name it, or meet it in a particular room, then do so; however, it is important that you make the space, take the time and walk the cat back. And remember, if you don't feel successful at finding the root of your fear when you use this process, don't beat yourself up. Just come at it again with fresh intent the next time…and the next…and the next.

Love or Fear Scouts

Every experience or thought affords the opportunity to either extend love or share fear. The way to understand it is simple. If you follow your emotions upstream, which means back to their origination as we have discussed, you will find they are motivated by either love (a sense of community, unity and sharing), or by fear (anxiety, concern, paranoia or worry). Understanding which motivated your action is important because not only will it change the nature of your personal experiences, it will also guide you out of your illusion and into your awakening.

For example, Chris leaves for the county fair to ride the Ferris wheel. She loves riding Ferris wheels and finds them completely exhilarating. She loves the view from the top, the music, the people all having fun, and can't wait to get there. Her experience will most likely be great; her journey is prompted by joy. On the other hand, Pat has promised his son he'd take him on the Ferris wheel at the county fair. He has always hated rides; he doesn't like the smells there or crowds of people. He especially hates it when other riders rock the seats and make him dizzy. His motivation to ride is obligation, which upstream is fear of rejection or fear of being perceived as a neglectful parent. Most likely, his experience will also be what he expects: unpleasant. In both cases, their scouts ran ahead energetically announcing their arrival. In the first case, Chris may have gotten all the lights green, her gas tank was full and found five dollars on the ground. In Pat's case, he had to wait for a train that seemed to take forever, he spilled coke on himself in his impatience as he waited, and then discovered he had forgotten his wallet at home. Fear scouts set the mood energetically.

Ahead of you then go fear scouts or love scouts, depending upon who sent them. The love scouts go ahead energetically saying, "I'm coming and I'm bringing love and joy, sharing and connection." Doors fly open, and people you haven't met yet are already receptive to you. They await your coming. It is as if someone greased the wheels in the big machinery for you. People are more friendly, accepting and eager to assist in unforeseen ways. It feels as if things are going your way. We've all had similar experiences but never really knew why.

When fear scouts precede you, you're sending the energy of fear, smallness and anxiety to prepare your coming. Consequently, you find many doors shut tightly upon your arrival. No one graciously welcomes you. Most people feel uncomfortable with fear energy, because that energy triggers their own personal fears. They shut you out and your scout too. It seems the world is against you.

Looking upstream from an emotion is how you identify whether your action or thought is motivated by fear or love. As with walking the cat back, we are looking for motivation. We want to see who has set up camp in our thought process. Looking upstream simply means, you identify what prompted what, which then prompted what, which is now why you feel angry or guilty. Anger is not a root emotion; it is a secondary one. If you feel angry, start asking, "why?" Keep going back. Are you angry because something cost more than you thought it should? Is it because some service you received was inferior to the standard you expected? Now, what does that have to do with either fear or love? Keep going upstream to the source or root fear. Why do you feel it is so important to get a good deal? Is it to get more and pay less? Is it because you fear running out of money if you let every Tom, Dick and Harry take advantage of you? Now you're moving upstream to the root. Perhaps you fear being destitute, unsupported, broke, humiliated relying on welfare. Maybe this fear of lack is the motivation.

Imagine that you want a specific car. You especially want one within your comfortable price bracket, with the miles you've allocated as acceptable, and within a fairly close geographical area. All your efforts to find one are simply not panning out. Every time you find one that fits that bill, it is already sold. You simply meet endless frustration. Let's look upstream. What needs to change in your world to accomplish your goal of procuring your desired vehicle?

Imagine sitting behind the wheel of this specific car in the color that would please you most, with the price you're happiest to pay. How do you feel, not just superficially, but as you drive it, and as you fill it with fuel? Do you feel overjoyed, enthusiastic, like a young kid or a successful person? Do you feel weighted; suddenly overwhelmed with payments that make you question your ability to consistently meet them? Do you feel stupid for following a whim because the upkeep or fuel demands are higher than you want to pay? If you look upstream into your core motivation, you will see why no vehicles of your specific parameters are available. If your motivation is fear of any kind, of lack or regret or support, your doors will remain closed.

Do you *really* want that car? Do you really love the vehicle, and how it looks, sounds, and feels on the road with you behind the wheel? How do you feel about driving it? Stop there. Reallocate your energy into love. That reallocation may require some work, removing beliefs that everything falls apart when you have what you want. It may require releasing some outdated beliefs of self-worth or guilt, but therein lies the key to doors flying open.

Let's say you have a party. Imagine the difference in results if you are motivated by a desire to bring people together in a spirit of connectedness and joy (love) versus feelings of obligation or guilt (fear of reprisal). In other words, you get together because that is what you love to do, or you feel obliged to have a party for your friends because they had one for you. You can feel it in your cells. One party is joyful and fun and no one wants to leave, whereas the other one is poorly attended, the food tastes terrible, no one brought dessert, and it's a struggle to find anything interesting to talk about.

Every action, thought and word is motivated by either fear or love. Consider going to work or school. When you have something to look forward to that you enjoy (in joy = love), the day flies by with little conscious effort. Conversely, when you have to drag yourself out of bed after hitting the snooze button three times, everything goes wrong. You encounter red lights, detours on the way to work, more delays and problems once at work, sour weather, missed lunch. They all have their roots in the attacking energy of fear. There's the fear of being fired if you miss work, the fear of being homeless if you get fired, and ultimately survival fears of life and death if you are homeless.

What about when two travel together who hold conflicting energies, one of love and one of fear? The unfortunate natural response is that as both scouts go ahead of them, most people will respond by shutting their doors. Even though one rider is a friendly, they *must* lock the door against the other. It may then feel like fear is more powerful than love, and is capable of countering it. However, if fear is riding along, adjustments will be made in that situation to protect oneself. The thing to realize is that fear *is* attacking energy. It may not seem like it. It may even feel harmless to the one exuding it, but it always attacks the unity, the oneness of true nature, the True Nature of our Beingness.

However, if the commitment to love is unwavering and confident, which means it is the predominant energy vibration of your being, it doesn't matter who accompanies you and what they bring with them energetically. Your open and loving energy will provide the trust others need to open the door for you both. Your intense love can handle the others' paltry fears. The vibration of love is stronger than fear, as it is stronger than anything; it is the life-giving source of creation in existence. Most people, however, begin to resonate with the vibration of fear. It is convincing and attractive, as odd as that may sound. It bonds people together superficially. So until you can commit your entire being to love, your own fears and the fears of those who accompany you will participate in creating your reality.

Perhaps you are familiar with Thoreau's quote, "Nothing is so much to be feared as fear," or perhaps you remember President

Franklin D. Roosevelt's, "The only thing we have to fear is fear itself." This concept is not new. The distractions surrounding the base fear are what prevents you from conquering it. But once you recognize the original fear and shine the light on it, it is no longer a fear lingering in the darkness. It is like a real child in need of love and comfort, and generally, that is all that is required for dissolving fears. Fighting fears is not appropriate because the motivation is fear. It is fear of the prevailing fear, or fear that the fear will overcome you.

> *Yet any attempt to resolve the basic conflict through the concept of mastery of fear is meaningless. In fact, it asserts the power of fear by the simple assumption that it need be mastered. The essential resolution rests entirely on the mastery of* **love**.
> – *A Course in Miracles*

When you continue to choose love as the motivator of your thoughts and actions, your experiences will reflect that conscious decision. You will feel that the wheels are being greased for you and it's no wonder others call you blessed. As the nature of your experiences continue to shift into more love-based experiences, you will begin to understand and know the meaning of awakening. It is simply living more fully in love instead of fear. *A Course in Miracles* teaches just that, as the quote in the chapter heading states, "Essentially all healing is a release from fear."

"If you bring forth what is within you, what you bring forth will save you. If you do not bring forth what is within you, what you do not bring forth will destroy you."

– St. Thomas Logian

13 Everyone is an Aspect of Self

One of the most challenging things the ego world perpetuates is the need to be different or separate. On one hand, it is how you identify your individuality, and on the other, it is what keeps you estranged. Part of the awakening process, although it doesn't have to actually be a process, is the realization or the knowing that we are all connected, or all One. This belief sounds very Eastern in thinking and foreign to Western minds. In theory, it sounds delightfully esoteric, but in practice it is usually distasteful.

What needs to happen is a transformation in the way you view others. Instead of seeing them as human bodies separate and distinct from your human body, you need to transform your perceptions and see others as simply the same as you, a vehicle manifested for the journey home. By doing so, you focus less on the vehicle they are driving and more on the driver within. To begin this transformation, start with something fairly simple. It will transform the way you see and provide an opportunity for healing. You are going to learn how everyone can be seen as an aspect of yourself. When you recognize that others appear in your life because you draw them there, or create them, then you recognize that you are creating your own illusion. You also learn that if they contain some aspect of you, your willingness to see them as being one with you isn't such a far stretch.

Magic Mirror

Imagine that you were shown a mirror in which you could see the particular traits you most needed to work on: what you most need to release to return to your native, or spirit state. Imagine the mirror also showed you the traits you most wanted to embody: shifting your personality to embody that spiritual entity you always have been, allowing you to return to your natural peaceful, loving Self. Would you believe what you witnessed in the mirror, avoid it, or smash it to pieces? At one time or another, I suppose we've all responded in each of the three ways.

The mirror simply reflects everyone you know: your friends, family, co-workers. To understand this statement, start with someone you like, perhaps a good friend. First identify what you like most about them. Rather than a superficial trait, find what makes them important to you. What makes you gravitate to them even though you may not agree on everything? When you boil it down, what makes them unique in your bag of friends? What is the trait that you most value and would miss the most if you were to lose this friend? What you are looking for is an aspect of their Highest Self that reflects an aspect of *your* Highest Self. It is the trait that you either want to embody or could integrate into your own healing, consciously or not.

Hold your best friend in your mind's eye. You consider all the obvious traits first: kind, generous, loving, supportive, intuitive. Then you think, with eyes shut, if this person were to leave my life, what would be the unique thing I would miss about them the most? And there it is, the reflection of your Highest Self mirrored for you.

In my case, my dear friend is the bridge between the physical and metaphysical worlds. She always seems to reach in somewhere and pull out an inspiration from a divine source especially for me, at just the right time. I know it must be coming from some non-physical source because it fits my current quandary so well. Without guidance from some other plane of existence, she couldn't have planned the timing herself. There it is. She verifies guidance for me, makes me feel less alone in my struggle to find wisdom, and sometimes it's just nice to hear it from *outside* my head.

She is an example of what I need to embody myself. Someday she *won't* be in my life, as we all change vehicles sooner or later. When that happens, will I be left grieving her loss and feeling I have been abandoned to this physical world alone, or will I have embodied the trust to connect with metaphysical guidance myself? Can I take her lead and find the bridge myself? Her gift to me was not just to grace me with her translation abilities, but also to shine a way that it not only is possible, but can be done quite easily. It is not a coincidence that this attribute is one that is a prerequisite along my specific journey.

Let's try this process with someone else. It is really quite simple once you begin to apply the principles to everyone you know. Let's take a sibling, a sister or someone you have known your whole life. This may seem a little harder. What is the trait that provides a mirror to your Highest Self? If you have ever had a sister or friend who has been challenged with cancer, you may have had a chance to identify this trait already. When the possibility is lurking that they may not be around much longer, the person suddenly becomes more precious to you. Imagine this person leaving your life forever. What is the unique trait that you feel you cannot live without? Of course you will consider all the physical things like not being able to do things together, not being able to call her up, not being able to see her laugh or feel her hug, but go beneath all that. What is the unique trait that makes her so special to you?

Does she bring the sunshine with her wherever she goes? Maybe that is what it is. And how valuable is that? Infinitely valuable. Can you imagine her never coming to see you on a sad and gloomy day and not feeling her bright energy and sunshiny smile? Do you need to embody more of that kind of energy? Do you carry heavy or grief-filled energy too often? Do you worry too much, carrying the burdens of others as if it would help them lighten their load by doing so? It doesn't help others when you carry their loads too. It just increases both your loads. Maybe you need to put down all the heaviness, unclothe, so to speak, and lie naked in the sunshine giggling!

This attribute of your sister, or whomever, is one you may want to embody or at least remember when life gets you down or you find yourself carrying a heavy burden in dreary darkness. Bring on the sunshine! Bring on a smile! Be a radiant example to others that lightness is simply there for the asking. You see, we're not looking for the most complicated thing imaginable, only the perfect simplicity of the gift of their Highest Self.

Now think of someone else in your life. Wade through all the obvious traits of this person until you uncover the unique thing that makes them particularly special to you. Keep in mind that this task is not a group assignment, because the very same person can inspire each person in their life in a wholly different way. It is through *your* eyes only that your reflection in the mirror can be seen.

Now let's look at the Lower Self. What does this same person mirror for you, which instead of being a trait you want to embody, is something you want to eliminate? For example, what consistently bothers you the most about this person? Again, it's not the superficial things like being late or not being tidy, but what is the underlying trait that you are always aware of, that you overlook because you care about this person so much? The lesson here is one taught through the teaching methods of the Lower Self, which means on a more base level. You've found the Higher Self lesson, but being diligent students, you don't want to miss anything, so look deeper. What is the Lower Self message?

Think about the good friend we started with. She has this wonderful quality of being able to translate from the physical to the metaphysical world, but she also nitpicks. She is articulate and chooses her words thoughtfully, part of the job of a good translator, but she also scrutinizes every word you speak. "Do you mean, literally, that?" She doesn't give you any slack to speak generally. She doesn't let the littlest thing go without comment or recognition. It is her challenge to find a balance in her life between being an excellent translator, having all resources available, and letting life happen fluidly with the people she loves. What is your challenge here? She is reminding you that on the course you signed up for, you need to let some line out. Don't reign in so tightly. Allow others their own mistakes. Don't nitpick. Now, whether we learn our lesson solely depends upon whether or not we follow the guidance and institute it in our lives. Finding the message is pretty easy.

Let's look again at your sibling, Miss Sunshine! What a lovely Higher Self she embodies for you. What does her Lower Self have for you as well? Perhaps she does lots of funny quirky things that sometimes matter and sometimes don't, but what is the main thing? Maybe she is judgmental of people who don't fit her philosophies or paradigm. The more someone agrees with your core philosophies of life and how to live, the more you like them; but if they live *outside* your belief system, then you don't like them as much or at all. This judgment concerns accepting people as they choose to be, exactly how they choose to act, and wherever they are along their journey. That's a nice message to receive, but do you want to hear it again and again, while pointing a finger outside yourself, saying in righteous judgment, "Look, *they* are judgmental"?

Each person in your life holds a mirror to you. You'll receive many messages at different times in your life, but if you could just look for *one* message from the others' Higher Self and *one* from their Lower Self, you would afford yourself many wonderful opportunities to release or reclaim. What about the messages you have for others? No doubt you have messages for others, but that is none of your business. It has literally nothing to do with you.

The purpose here is two-fold. Not only are you being given a valuable message for the advancement of your soul, but you are being given an opportunity to see that we are all the same, all connected in Oneness. It simply means that the stuff we are made of, our core essence, is the same. It is the life giving energy of the universe, the vibration of unconditional love. To know that truth is one thing, but to *know* it with every cell of your being is another. When you are capable of looking at another and seeing this mirror gift they hold for you, you are seeing a part of *you*. It's not a reflection of you, but actually a part of you. You share the same Highest Self. Your Highest Self and someone else's Highest Self is the same being, the same information, the same energy. How you hear it and translate it is specific to you, and how you communicate and see things is yours also, but the essence is the exact same fabric. When you connect with someone and see these aspects of yourself in your friends and even adversaries, you are able to touch the part of each other that is this Oneness. You also can find the compassion needed to forgive or allow, as you recognize that you embody attributes that you judge others as having. In fact, as is so often the case, the very things we judge people most harshly on are the ones we continue to exhibit but of which we are still unaware. However, when people tell you what *your* issue is, remember you are just being *their* mirror.

You can even take it a step further. You can imagine that this world was created by you, for you. That means, this person you love who is your friend as well as this person who is your Achilles' heel are both aspects of you. They were created by you, sent by your mind, or your larger Mind, to see a part of you that you cannot see yourself.

Mercury Theory

What if only you exist? What if this illusion consisted of only one entity and many actors, playing many parts? Indulge me with this thought. Have you ever seen the chemical element mercury? Its properties are quite unique. It acts as one semi-liquid glob, but if it gets splattered, it can become a thousand tiny liquid globs, all rolling around trying to find their mates. They will all congeal again into one glob if they are still moving. Their nature is to return to the original uniglob state. Mercury is like that.

If you have ever seen an old thermometer drop and break, you can remember the distinct quality of mercury. For a moment, think of us as one big glob of mercury, that became separated long ago. Some of us flew off into what feels like oblivion. That would be the mercury that got lodged behind the couch in the dark and dust. Some of us landed in the dirt and collected a bunch of grit and sand with our mercury. Some didn't fall far from the thermometer and are clean but a few shards of glass are intermixed. And some were shattered into such tiny pieces, that it's a wonder that any mercury remained. But still, we're all like the element that we call mercury. We would inherently like to reunite.

Herein lies the problem. Instead of knowing that we are the mercury—which of course is my analogy for the Divine—we believe we are separated and distinct individuals. Really, we came from the same soul thermometer, just shattered into a billion pieces. No matter how small the quantity or what we have collected along our journey, we are still made of the very same, in fact, *exact* material. Can it then be said that we are all One? We've become separated, playing out individual roles in private dreams, but essentially we are the *same* piece of shattered mercury, or separate pieces of the divine.

So, when you see yourself in someone else, you *really* are seeing yourself in them. I mean you are really seeing yourself, just maybe a part of you that needs synthesizing, cleaning or correcting. One day, or on another realm, we will all fit back together into the original mercury blob. If we all went back with our dirt and dust, grime and glass, we would not be the original thing again. We would be something in addition, something that would then no longer fit into the thermometer.

I like to look at it this way. If you want to return to your original state of divinity you must fit into the space you want to occupy. And it's not really a space, it's a vibration. You want to be light, but you are carrying a heavy load. How will you fit all this luggage into the trunk of a VW? You can't. Dump the baggage and you can easily fit. Simply without judgment, only the quality of your pure nature must be reattained to return. All these mirror and mercury analogies are simply to help you find a way to transform your perceptions and see what you are *not*, so you can become aware of *what you are.*

Mirror, Mirror on the Wall

If you have chosen to see others as an aspect of yourself, and you see what they have to offer you, when do they stop annoying you? When you actually are able to embody your Highest Self in relation to what they are offering you. In other words, *they* are not going to get it until *you* get it. If they are essentially an unhealed or disintegrated part of *you*, then *they* are not changing until *you* do.

For example, if someone close to you, let's take your spouse, cannot ever relax, is never at peace, and is constantly restless, waiting for *them* to find tranquility for *you* to find tranquility is not an option. I know it feels like your life would be immeasurably more peaceful if they just relaxed, but I suggest that they won't. Accepting them as they are is a lovely idea; however, if you peg your own peace on someone else's state of mind, something else needs to happen. You have to look at your *own* lack of peace. Maybe next to your spouse you seem very relaxed, but alone and as an isolated individual taken out of context of the relationship, what would you see? Do you feel totally at peace now? Relax your body. Breathe. Do you still feel restlessness in there somewhere? Now sit with a feeling of inner peace, or at least what a semblance of inner peace might feel like. Is your spouse a distraction or a reasonable excuse to delay the search for genuine tranquility?

This *other* is *you*. He is simply a part of you, that has come to life. He is the embodiment of your own issue. Therefore, waiting for your own personal twin to become something or someone else, or embody tranquility or peace, could take a very long time.

I suggest, as you can probably figure by now, that the mirror on the wall or in your bed is there to show you exactly what you need to do in order to take the next step on your personal journey home. The great thing about having a living testament to your efforts right there under your nose is that true results are unfortunately all that matter. Intentions and attempts won't change a thing. Have you ever tried to work on some mechanical thing, a toaster or a car? The thing simply will not work unless you have corrected what is keeping it from working. You can't just jiggle, unscrew things and hope and pray, because unless you have affected the very thing that is broken, it won't come to any avail. The same can be said about our mirrored selves.

So now, your *spouse's* restlessness is no longer an issue for you, in so far as it is still there, it shows you that *you* still are restless. Finding peace is a direct way to Awaken, so it is no small matter. It is obviously paramount to the place where you are right now. What stands between you and inner peace is *not* your malcontented husband, but your *own* unwillingness to find peace yourself. The process, however, is a solo journey. The only role your partner plays in this restless issue is as an indicator. When his restlessness no longer bothers you, and that is the key, it is no longer a block to your own peace, and you know that issue has been integrated. His role now becomes something else. Do you dare to peek in the mirror again?

Let's look at another example. Most adults can relate to this example from one side of the fence or the other, or both. The topic is extra-marital affairs. First, let's have a look at the mirror of the socially accepted offended partner, the one not actually having the affair. What aspect of you is your mate mirroring back? Look beyond the obvious. You may never have physically stepped out on your mate, so how can you see this?

Let's start with a few questions. In the relationship where you felt cheated on, did you have all arms and legs inside the vehicle? Had you closed off all other possibilities to others in that relationship? Did that bother you? Do you wear your ring and tell others you are happily involved, while looking out the corner of your eye at others as potential mates? Is part of you unwilling to completely commit to avoid pains in the heart area? Do you see where I am going with this? Your mate may only be illustrating in living color what may be happening only cerebrally for you. You may think that what goes on in your head has absolutely no effect on the actions that someone *else* may take, but I challenge that thinking.

View it as *your* play! Every actor on your stage is an aspect of you, just as every character in a book is some part of the author, realized or not. Very likely the person who cheated on you also cheated on another partner long before you were even having thoughts in your brain about being committed. That is generally the case. For example, if an actor or actress were cast in a comedy role and became popular as a comedian, they would probably be recast in other comedy roles in other pieces. They are good at comedy roles. Some people attract certain issues, since they are so good at mirroring those. You just chose a very qualified and professional actor for your life's play, no amateurs are cast here.

Returning to the affair, the question becomes, "How do I cease the drama (it does *not* feel like a comedy right now) and grow out of this particular phase?" First, scanning the self for open doors is of primary importance. If you are looking for an excuse to move out of the relationship, have the courage to step out the front door and walk on down the street. For argument's sake, suppose you feel a strong connection to this person, a deep love and potentially much to gain or learn. The mirror will hang there until you choose to close your own doors of potential possibilities.

You step into the library of infinite resources and ask yourself if *this* person, in *this* life is the one for you. You weigh your options. Play out some of your other possible scenarios to the end, or after 10 years. One of my friends years ago told me, "Don't get divorced, every guy comes with his own baggage. At least with the first one you already know what his is. You get married again, you just have to start over." How would another option be different and what is keeping you from committing to this one person? Do you still like this person? Do you respect him? Do you even want to be with her? Are you waiting for your fairy godmother to come, or for everything to be perfect, or the time you don't have any financial stress, or him or her to quit that job?

If you have the inability to commit (and commitment is a required trait for keeping the focus to return Home), you will see yourself in one mirror after another until you find the ability to embody commitment. That is, *if* commitment is what you are working on right now. It doesn't have to be commitment to a person, but that is an excellent way to work on commitment. It can be commitment to a cause, a dream, a belief or whatever you seek. Each path to commitment comes complete with its own challenges.

After you decide to channel your energetic resources into one person, cause, or belief, the doors simply close. It is similar to a long hallway filled with many doors on each side. If you stop to open and experience what is in each room, you may never reach the door at the end of the hall. If only one door is present at the end of the hall, all resources can be funneled to that end. Truthfully, you are the only one who knows if this life is about attaining the door at the end of the hall. You will find that when you close off options, other people will sense these new boundaries and respond to you in a different way. Similarly, when your door was open, others could peek in out of curiosity simply because it was open. When you focus and commit to your choices, life becomes simpler; you have more energy for the mission as the mission becomes defined. Then, the mirror begins to reflect something else and you see *another* aspect of yourself.

When you can see others as an aspect of you, you suddenly take the separateness and distinctness out of the distance between you. You have been them and they, you. You created them for you, they created you for them, and yet you are both aspects of one united Being. The mind cannot completely comprehend this idea, because we are bred to understand things through the ego's interpretation. The more you work through prejudices and preconceptions, the more this understanding will not only feel right, you will then realize that others have everything to do with you.

Embracing Versus Resisting

Another way of finding the connection to others that leads to healing is through embracing them versus resisting them. This prospect may feel counter intuitive or simply not acceptable, because your ego self will demand that you disconnect from them and change your phone number. Amazingly, however, it actually leads to your own healing.

No doubt you have tried letting go of something or someone that bothers you, only to feel them still pulling on you energetically. The letting go usually only works if you no longer have any attachment, and all emotion has been drained from the situation or person. But the reason this thing or person bothers you is because strings are still connecting you to the very thing that annoys you. If you have tried to let it go and find that it just drifts behind you like a balloon tied to your ankle, then you know you need to try something else. Your first thought will be to push it away, but it will just bounce back if it is still tied at your ankle and you will encounter it again and again.

The secret is to take the one that annoys you most and embrace them energetically. You need not be near them physically. Let's say you have a person with whom you have reached your level of tolerance. She is pushy and annoying and you feel certain she is using you. She keeps asking you for assistance until you reach the point where it is not okay; it is creating resentment and you can only think about her in a negative way. How do you bring her in or embrace her? First, you *identify her by name and turn that name into an aspect of you.* Her name is Tina and she is now going to be seen as some aspect of you. This part can be uncomfortable.

Second, you *see Tina not how she presents herself to you now, but through her tender heart.* You speculate about how she came to choose this guise you now witness as her manifest self. You see her life as a child, perhaps a young girl who was unloved by her mother, abused by her stepfather, or felt left out in a family not entirely blood-related. Do not think of her as a separate being, you simply step into Tina shoes and imagine what may or may not have transpired to create this physical Tina. You are softening to the part of her that you may never have known, but that part that led to the attributes that annoy you now. Continue along this line, allowing for understanding of why she annoys you so much, how her need for acceptance may have led her to feel the need to seem bigger than others, and how her loneliness as a child may have led her to believe she needed to assert herself more strongly to be included or loved. As her affected behavior comes from wanting to be loved so badly, she will try whatever she can to receive what she feels she does not have. You are beginning to wear your Tina shoes, and suddenly, you feel touched that she is such a fragile human being and is trying so hard to connect soul to soul. *A Course in Miracles* says that any attack is simply a call for love.

Speaking to a writer's workshop, I walked the participants through this exercise in order to show them how to deal with causes of writer's block. Frequently, an obsession with a negative and unresolved personality (present or past) can wrangle away too much creative energy and leave you feeling empty and unable to be access your creativity. One woman offered her challenging example for the rest of the group. She admitted to us that her block was a woman named Lynn who was her daughter's oncologist. She said that Lynn's behavior was condescending and it made her feel she was not hearing the truth about her daughter's cancer. She felt stupid around the doctor and also that Dr. Lynn's comments did not seem genuine.

As a group we decided to step into Lynn's shoes. First of all, we all wanted to step right back out, not wanting to deal with cancer all day and having to tell people their loved ones were going to die. Sympathy chord number one was struck. Next, we imagined her day. We imagined her hours. We imagined her wanting to change jobs but feeling she couldn't leave because of the loans she owed to pay her schooling. Then we saw the reason for the happy face that appeared unauthentic to our writer. We imagined Lynn getting up early to do her hospital rounds, dreading to tell this young mother that her daughter had a slim chance of being alive in 5 years, or even that she required chemotherapy or radiation. Somehow it was easier telling folks who had already had a rich and full life that they had cancer, even though it couldn't be easy at all. She knew it was her job, but underneath the fake smile was a very sensitive woman with a daughter of her own. Pretty soon, our whole group wanted to send sympathy flowers to Dr. Lynn. Before long, the writer said it changed her whole perspective of the doctor, and the feeling of being stupid was replaced by a softness accompanied by sympathy. She saw that the doctor probably never intended to seem fake or condescending.

Next, look at those common traits that led your nemesis to exhibit unintended behavioral traits. Returning to Tina, look at everything she has brought with her as you welcomed her into your soul home. She brought all her fears too. You may not have the same ones, so they may not feel like fear, but you can soothe them if you identify them as common and unnecessary fears. To heal yourself is to heal others, so as you heal her, you heal you and vice versa. What is the predominant trait that you feel as you welcome her in, and you whole-heartedly embrace her? You may have thought that her habit of using you bugged you most; however, as you welcome her in, it seems more like compensation for her feeling of not belonging or not being accepted that holds the most energy. Examine that possibility, in her and in you, because at this time, you are the same. What is going on in your life right now to make you feel unaccepted? Are you putting something out there and your subliminal fear is that it won't be received as you expected? Is your expectation of acceptance not happening as you had hoped? What is happening in your relationships or job or creative life that feels like non-acceptance? The answer is what Tina is about for *you*.

There is no separation. It only appears that way when you see her through the eyes of the ego illusion. To bring her in, you heal her by soothing her, acknowledging with your heart that she is accepted. Perhaps her acceptance is not the way she has expected, but transfer the understanding that she is accepted in more whole, complete ways that speak of our innate divinity. She heals you as you process this awareness for her in your mind. We are no different really, in the end, or rather, in the beginning. We express ourselves in very different ways, but if we all go looking far enough, we find the same sorts of fears, paranoia and desires to be loved and to have someone to love. Resisting, fighting and ignoring only draw that kind of energy to us more intensely. Find the place where you share vulnerabilities, and that is the place in your heart that can open up for healing and forgiveness.

"Love is God in manifestation, and the strongest magnetic force in the universe. Pure, unselfish love draws to itself its own; it does not need to seek or demand."

– Florence Scovel Shinn

14 Choosing Love and Forgiveness

Unconditional Love—*Divove*

The English word *love* has many meanings. The meaning I want to talk about is the least understood variation of love and yet it is the only true love. It is unconditional love. It has nothing to do with the physical body or personal relationships. It is the energy or vibration of the essence of creation energy. You may think of love as meaning the way you feel about someone or something, but that type is conditional and is more akin to words such as lust, need, obligation, duty, loyalty, and protective or brotherly love. To use a wholly different word is desirable here. Allow me to introduce a new word—*Divove*—which is a combination of the words divine and love. Divove is something that most humans have never experienced and trying to describe it is like trying to describe the taste of licorice to someone who has never tasted it. However, it is worth the attempt!

Divove is an essence of being, not necessarily a feeling or an emotion, but it will consume the space in your being where emotions usually reside. It is generated from your core self, your genuine being, your most divine self. That explanation may not help since most of us aren't wholly familiar with the divine essence I speak of. First, it might help to describe what it's not. Divove is *not* the love you have for a child or parent or someone in need. It *is* the love you have for someone you don't know that overcomes you with concern and care, but you don't know why. It has no strings attached and no judgment or feelings of responsibility. It is *not* the physical attraction you have for someone that makes you feel tingly just to look upon their body and face. It is *not* the love you have that ever includes the word *should*, as in, I should love this person because she is my mother, or I should love this person because he is my son.

It is not any kind of love that contains conditions, as with, "I will love you if you love me back; I will love you as long as you don't love anyone else at the same time; I will love you as long as you do what I want you to do; I will love you as long as you are quiet." Divove is different. It is the essence of deep care beyond anything rational. For example, if you were sitting in a train and a teenage boy were sitting in the seat ahead of you, to experience Divove with him would be to watch his restlessness and discomfort and gently want to place your hand on his head and heal all wounds of dis-ease and conflict. It would be your desire to help him find a comfortable place to lay his head, to simply open your heart and pour out this essence of divove so strongly it would be like offering a cup of strong, black coffee to a groggy night owl who was forced to get up with the sun.

Divove is not reasonable. It is not about *having* to love someone. It is loving them in spite of themselves. Also it is not about loving someone just because no one else can or will, or because you aspire to be a Mother Teresa. No martyrdom exists in divove nor any guilt or condescension, only deep and true equality of souls. It is not feeling sorry for someone. If you see someone passing in the street who is legless in a wheelchair, you may open your heart and pour out compassion, but more than likely it will be tainted with feelings of pity. Divove is a state of mind, not a feeling. It is a deep knowing who you are and it is not something that turns on or off. It is like being an optimist or a pessimist; it is generally your outlook or way of being. Experiencing divove changes you. You cannot go back, nor would you want to.

Divove is the most powerful love. You may think you have felt love in moments of lustful ecstasy, and indeed that is a very powerful emotion, but in a different way. Lust is very personal. It is directed at you and no one else is feeling it. With lust there is another who is responsible for the feeling. And it definitely is a feeling, not a state of being, because for anyone who has ever experienced this, you know it is anything but permanent. Divove, however, is more like the feeling that may overcome you when you happen onto a meadow in the mountains that has just come into bloom. The moment is irreplaceable as the sun comes out from behind a cloud exposing tiny mountain flowers of all colors and varieties, and you feel they are blooming just for you. You suddenly feel alive and in love with life. That is divove.

This divine love is not personal though. It is a state of being, and has nothing to do with whether anyone is receiving it or not. It is creation energy unleashed, flowing through you with no locks or passwords, no dams or detours, just simple, unabated creation energy doing what it does. So if you were using the word divove in a sentence, it would not require a direct object, like the word love does. For example, I love you. I love who? You. I love ice cream. I love what? Ice cream. A direct object. But divove is not like that. It would simply be, *I divove*. Are you divoving today? Don't you enjoy divoving? Can you teach me how to divove? If you are in the state of beingness where divove resides, everyone and everything in your world receives this energy by default. By the very nature of divove, you cannot or would not turn it off, choose to bestow it only on some and not others or in any way be selective about who divove energy falls onto. The sun radiates light. We may feel it is shining on us, but it is simply in a state of shining. When you divove, you shine on all around you without exclusion. To understand it in another way, it is very much like being depressed. When you are genuinely depressed, you cannot pretend or be joyful and happy around some people and not around others. Your state of being depressed falls on all who enter your world. You weren't depressing Bill or Nancie, you were just in a state of being depressed. That's how it is with Divove. It is a state of being.

Now how do you arrive at this state of being and why would it be so desirable? First of all, if you have ever experienced this divine love for even a split second, you would never have to ask why. It is a state of kindness, of such peace, belonging, and feeling totally okay about everything that you want to live in it forever. Your chest expands and feels like it is taking in the whole known world and everything in it. Everyone is being sucked into your chest, to be adored and nurtured and cared for. And it really doesn't matter if they reject you, if they know about being divoved, or if they are even likable; you just feel at peace with everything.

About the *how*, it is not just about practicing, it is about finding out who you are and *believing* it! It is truly that simple, and that concept is what this book is all about: helping you to remember who you are, and liking it. Having a word for this love will help you understand that it exists, and it will offer you a specific image and allow you to recognize it once you have experienced it.

Forgiveness and Judgment

Walking hand in hand with divove is forgiveness. It is a by-product of being loving as well as a course of action to aid it. First, it is important to know that forgiveness is *not* done for someone else, and it is *not* about condoning what someone else has done or said. It is only a way to free *yourself.* That's all. It is a gift you give to yourself. No one else really needs to know about it, and yet, they will feel it when it happens.

Second, forgiveness is not about reexamining your big ledger listing everyone's misdeeds and then condescending to draw a line through one, only to come back later and squint through the scratch to remember again. It is about getting the big pink eraser out and rubbing it out altogether. You may want to come back later and sift through those old familiar wounds, but they won't be there. And condescending to forgive isn't forgiveness; it is condescension.

Third, forgiveness is a divine concept, therefore, you may reach a point when you have truly given everything and simply cannot find it on your heart to forgive. You may still feel justified in holding a grudge. All is not lost. If you have the *willingness* to forgive, but cannot, then place the whole burden in a package containing all the misdeeds others have done (or you feel *you* have done) in the hands of the Divine. The rest will be done *for* you. Later when you peek back inside the package, it will be empty; the stomach-wrenching feelings will be gone, and only peace will remain.

Forgiveness lets you reopen a space in your heart for that person or yourself, and lets the light of love envelop and heal. Forgiveness is the greatest gift you can give yourself as you feel an expansive love replace a constricted wound.

If forgiveness is a spirit tool, realize that the ego has a tool it uses to counter it and it is judgment. The concept of forgiveness is not one that the ego would like you to embrace. In fact, the ego perpetuates separation in all ways, and when you forgive someone, the space between you and the other person gets smaller. The ego doesn't like that and will try to find sneaky ways to keep the separation. One of those ways is judgment.

Judgment is another way to provide the feeling of separation between you and others, whether they are individuals or groups of people. If I asked if you believed you were a judgmental person, your mind might quickly lean to the 'no' response. But consider what judgment entails. In a larger sense, you know it is not a desirable characteristic, and usually shows up with racism and bigotry. In a more local sense though, it shows up simply by you feeling that you know the answers that someone else doesn't, or feeling that people wouldn't have to be so unhappy if they could put into practice what they talk about. Even using your own self as a template to others is judgmental. If only they could have some self-discipline, or tone down their emotional responses, or not let their egotistical behavior get the best of them; essentially, if only they could be more like *you*. Or, using their same criteria in the other direction, if only you could become more like *them*.

What you are looking at is really another way of sabotaging your spiritual journey. To repeat the same responses again and again gets you nowhere. And when you judge others according to your standards, you are creating a chasm between others that cannot be filled. You are creating more separation. When you look at young people and make mental statements to the effect that, "They'll get it one day" or, "Don't they know that that behavior is destructive?" you are not honoring their process. When you look at someone you love and hold your judgment internally, pretending to be accepting and loving, but inside you are saying, "You spoiled brat, can't you get that under control?" you are still judging.

Let's lay something out here for clarity. Do you imagine that you are only responsible for what you *say* or *do*? Expand that sense of responsibility to include what you say, do, *think* and *feel.* In other words, you are responsible for everything about your world. Now when you look at judgment, it takes on a little different tone. Just because you are politically correct when others are around doesn't mean that, in your mind, you are not thinking heavily judgmental thoughts every time you pass someone who is darker or lighter skinned than you. I thought that it was bizarre, as a 6-year old artist, that people would discriminate according to the color of another. I naturally felt inferior because I only had one crayon to express my skin color, and it was a very boring color, when others got richer and more varied colors to express their skin. Then I was taught that one boring pale color was actually *good.* I was confused. It felt, even then, that someone was just making that up to compensate for the very boring, pale-tan color in the crayon box.

What things cause separation and what things create unity? The answer leads you to know which things are being generated from the ego and which from the spirit. This idea of forgiveness is huge, but we can't forgive someone with one hand and hold our noses when they pass with the other hand. Judgment is the way the ego can urge you to still keep a neutral space between you and others while feeling correct and spiritual because you have forgiven.

Judgment as a Method of Separation

Let's look at how judgment may be entering into your life, messing with your desire for unity and oneness. It does exactly the opposite, and here's how. You have a meeting with your child's teacher at school. You have decided to be civil and hear what the teacher has to say, even though you naturally are very protective about your own child. The teacher introduces some ideas about your child that you do not believe, and you feel that this teacher is showing how ignorant she is. You say all the placating words that make the teacher think you are being supportive when inside you are thinking, "What do they teach you people anyway?" And you leave feeling smug and superior because you are more intelligent, open-minded and creative at solving problems. What was the purpose? Was it to have a genuine interaction with another soul along your journey, or to get through a hassle as quickly as possible? Well, I have found that you deal with it now or deal with it later, but if it is in front of you, it will need to be dealt with. You may as well deal with it sooner and get it over with. And I don't mean dealing with the same experience with the same teacher, but facing the same energetic situation, and calling forth a new response from you.

Looking externally, you are a good mom or dad, attending to your child's behavior problems as seen through the eyes of the teacher and you behaved quite well when confronted. But let's eliminate the external aspect and fast-forward to the day that this teacher leaves the planet for another realm. Let's watch while she replays her life and is able to see every scene from the other person's viewpoint. She remembers that experience with you in the classroom. What she thought was a very productive meeting, she now sees was a sham. She sees you were placating her, diminutizing her in your mind, even as she spoke with such concern and compassion for your child. Stop the footage there.

If you could imagine that scenario, the time the other person in your interaction could see what you were truly thinking and feeling, then you might act very differently. Imagine that the other person really *can* hear what goes on in your mind, and *can* feel what you are feeling. Now, how do you feel, and what do you think? This exercise isn't just for the other person's sake, but for yours as well. How many times are *you* being made the fool, being told one thing while being judged as something entirely different?

Let's look at someone you love. Let's look at your child. You listen to the dreams and hopes of your vulnerable little one and say to yourself, "Yeah, I had those dreams too, kid, but life is gonna dash 'em." Don't you think the vibration of that thought has energy? It does. I am not suggesting that you lie as an option, or pretend to feel something that you don't. But let's look at your purpose: to bring unity and oneness to everything and everyone in your world. Instead of seeing the space in between, you see through the lens of your soul or your Higher Self. Instead of seeing Johnny as a smaller, limited version of you, imagine his Highest Self. Imagine him achieving his dreams, imagine being proud when it happens, and imagine telling others about it later. Let your mind go to a place bigger than your small mind can comprehend. Allow your mind to imagine that the thing is done, that his dream has been accomplished no matter how unlikely it may seem to your rational mind. Remember, the rational mind is a product of the ego to limit what you feel you are capable of doing in this life. Don't you think there is a vibration to *that* thought of infinite possibility? I assure you, Johnny knows it and feels it too.

You know what it feels like when you tell someone about a cool idea you have, hoping for some positive feedback or sharing of ideas, and the other person fakes enthusiasm? You hear the words and later replay them for encouragement, but they don't carry enough energy to power anything, much less your plan. You end up letting the idea fizzle, knowing in your heart that if so-and-so doesn't think it is feasible, then it must be stupid. Actually, you are just seeing your idea through someone *else's* eyes. That's all. What are they capable of in their own mind? That's what you have just been party to. What you are capable of at the largest scale, not according to the ego but according to the Divine, is greater than your imagination can handle. What is your Divine Right? What has been planned for you since before time? What prevents you from doing it?

It's important that you listen to someone without judgment, even if their opinions are as far from yours as possible. You honor their process. How they see things and who they portray is part of their bigger plan, or it wouldn't be happening. You honor their process even when it is someone you love and care about and they are being self-destructive. It is not for you to judge their behavior as wrong. If you haven't figured it out yet, there is no right or wrong, which actually makes the whole judgment thing a moot point anyway.

It's not your job to make sense of things, or to make them pleasant or turn them into a positive experience. You don't have to turn things into a paradise or utopia to accept them. Just know that the other person is having their personal spiritual journey too, and none of it may make any sense to either of you, but it's where you're all standing at any particular time. When you judge the other person for standing where they are standing, you have just placed a marker between the two of you. You become less close, which means, not only do you understand each other less, but a sense of lack of support permeates the experience; you have moved farther away from whatever your spirit is trying to move you toward. That thing that you are being moved toward is unity and peace. Those words sound lovely, and maybe even airy-fairy, but peace and unity possess energy, and that energy is the magic carpet that takes you Home. That means, anything that prevents that journey keeps you here, spinning around in the hamster wheel.

Going Home Together

Understanding the value of non-judgment is important because we are going Home together. "What? Why? Wait a minute. I'm responsible for myself and going Home when I am ready." Yeah, well, that's what I thought too, but we have been misinformed probably because we would have bailed out on the whole spiritual journey thing long ago if we thought we had to bring everyone else along.

Well, here's the best way I can describe this truth. *You are everything and everything is you.* Remember the old Stylistics song and all its remixes? I heard you singing it in your head. The group had a valid point if you are trying to grasp eternity. I see it like this. If we are God and God is us, then everyone else is God and God is them, right? Okay, so far so good. Then if we are God, any one of us can save the world. What I mean is, any one of us holds the key to bring the Sonship Home. That's a stretch. Let's try it this way. How are we ever going to connect and become One, the big *One* Buddha talked about, the *All are Children of God* that Christ talked about? We have to find a way to make us them and them us, right? We have to see others as an aspect of ourselves and also see God as an aspect of us both. We have to see ourselves as an aspect of others. This is the point where the space diminishes. Every living thing carries creation energy or it would cease to be living. The very energy that powers our little bodies, also powers the biggest rhinoceros and smallest beetle. That's how we are the same. Every living thing carries the memory of its creation, or its Creator. So if you go, I go. If I go, you go because, that's right, *we are the same*!

Stop looking for differences if you want to get off the wheel. Let the ego go unfulfilled, look for similarities, look at how someone is an aspect of you. Even the most unlikely person, if you think of what you do or don't like about them, is more than likely an aspect of you that is either healed or unhealed. This concept applies to every person, whether you know them or not, or you just admire them for some strange reason. You must carry the seeds of that strange reason or you would not be attracted to this person. Energy vibrations attract similar energy vibrations.

How do you have a real life interchange with people without judgment as your constant companion? I don't mean having interactions just with people of different colors, but with people who seem just like you. You see their Highest Potential, not their potential as history records it. You see their Divine Right, not your limited world rife with boundaries of safety as seen through your eyes only. You honor their journey, however different it may be from yours. You find the similarities in your plight; even though they may appear very different on the outside, the essence of them may be more similar than you think. You feel with your heart, not with your rational mind. The rational mind will tear this paragraph apart. It will say we *must* have standards, or people will think they can do anything. It will say we *must* judge others to keep ourselves knowing where we stand in relation. The rational mind will say a lot of stuff, but it will only be a lot of wonderful fuel for keeping the fires of separation alive and burning.

Let's look at your child's teacher again. Let her go on to her other realm now, but give her another scenario to take with her. Instead of the mental garbage with which you sat in judgment, imagine that throughout her dialogue of your child's problems, you only listened and held the image of her highest self in front of your mind's eye. You did not judge her words; you did not agree or disagree; you only opened your ears to hear what was not being said. You heard her own fears being projected onto your child, and you heard her own limitations being played out for Johnny. You heard her cry for unity, for support, for help, and you held only the highest image of what her Divine Right was. You didn't know specifically what that was, but only that it was much larger than she was exhibiting. *Then* on that day when she crossed over the barrier between this world and the next, she would see for an instant her Highest Self as held by you. Her heart would recognize that bigness and strive to reach it in whatever plane of existence she was entering next. What an empowering soul you have now become to her. What has it done for you?

Can you hold the image of another's Highest Self without coming to terms with your own? Eventually, your own Divine Self will want to have expression, breadth and expansiveness too. If you give this radiant image to others, aren't you giving it to yourself, an aspect of them? Or if you give it to you, do you not give it to others who are an aspect of you?

Can you look at the ones you love the most and not hold limiting images of them? Can you see anyone other than through your own limiting vision? Can you see those you love living without the standard of care and concern as elicited by the rational mind and society's rules and mores? Can you see destructive behavior as something other than destructive behavior? Can you see egotistical behavior as anything other than negative and constrictive? How do you rise above this response to something the spirit creates? You do it by looking through the lens of the Higher Self, by seeing someone's highest potential. You do it by finding your similarities and your vulnerabilities. You find your need to connect instead of segregate.

Think of your closest person. What do they do that makes you hold an internal dialogue with them of, "If only you could do this..."? What will it take to let the judgment go? Your journey is not their journey. No right or wrongs exist. Your path is not their path, and by honoring theirs, you honor your own. Try to see their situation through the eyes of the Divine; after all, you have the eyes of the Divine. Use them. You are God and God is you. You may not know what someone's Divine Self is, but just know that they have not been abandoned by our Creator and there is a plan for them as there is for every one of us. Let your vibration rise so that you see this beloved person as the highest they could be. An image will come in your mind, or a feeling of a grand or honorable One, or a wise and caring One, or a joyful, loving One. If you ask to see this person's Highest Self with your spiritual eyesight, you will be given an image to work with. That image will sustain you when you forget all about that Highest Self because you haven't seen evidence of it. That doesn't mean it isn't there, it only means they have not chosen to manifest it yet. Yet.

Now you are ready to truly forgive.

"We are what we think. All that we are arises with our thoughts. With our thoughts we make the world. Speak or act with a pure mind and happiness will follow you as a shadow, unshakable."

– Buddha

15 Dreaming an Illusion

Dreaming Within the Dream

Many people believe that dreams are just mental garbage collected from the day's overabundance of stimuli. That is certainly one interpretation, but dreams are also a powerful way to reveal the patterns in which we create our own personal illusions or holograms. Dreams are replete with little snippets of the most bizarre things: comments from a whole day's worth of conversations that develop a life of their own, deep fears repeated again and again in different ways, strange feelings that seem to have no origin, and figures long forgotten from the past. Trying to understand them in a literal way may not even be possible, nor may literal interpretation reveal the nature of dreams.

First of all, dreams illustrate for you a reality that appears real while you are dreaming, but becomes ethereal as you awaken and finally disappears as the day progresses. This is a metaphor for your spiritual journey. The hologram you have created appears

as a concrete reality while you are fully vested in it, but begins
to disintegrate as you start to see with other eyes and discover it
is mind-created. Then upon awakening, you find it was just a
dream, that it all could have been dreamed a different way, or it
could have been avoided all together.

Second, dreams provide the symbolism through which your
spirit can speak to you, showing you patterns and fears, areas of
growth happening, and places of stagnation.

Let's take a look at how you can reap the rewards of your
dream symbolism. Once again, as in the repeating theme of this
book, you created this illusion and only you can interpret it.
Everything in the dream is another aspect of you. The dreamer is
the dream and each participant in the dream. We have touched
on this a little already, but how do you learn and grow from this
knowledge?

As with the story of the man having nightmares about a
woman he loved, he needed to look at what she represented to
him, not to others, but only to him. When he found the answer,
he was able to interpret his dreams differently. Each time he was
doing something to this woman—berating her, chastising her,
or beating her—he could understand it as if he were doing these
things to his own joy (which is what she represented to him).
With this concept in mind, let's look at some archetypes and
their significances.

When you look into the dream world for symbolism, look
for larger concepts and emotions. Certain people will represent
authority to you: fathers, policemen, coaches, God, Santa Claus,
ministers, or teachers. Some people will represent insecurities:
those who have vulnerable information about you, those you
have previously loved but no longer trust, those who are trying
to undermine you or sabotage you in your mind. Look for areas
that represent fears. For some people it will be spiders, snakes,
scorpions, bears, or large scary men in black. Look for images of
falling, drowning, slipping, being unable to speak or run away,

feeling stuck in glue or molasses. These methods all speak to you about something that wants to be healed or needs correction.

Next, you need to look at the figures and consider your relationship to them in the dream. What do they represent to you and how are you reacting? This is going to be your key. If you are constantly having dreams where you are slipping, or there is a real threat to your safety, see how you respond. If you gleefully jump off the precipice you are dangling from, you probably aren't having issues with support. However, if you are sweating bullets trying to keep yourself clinging on to firm ground, it might be some kind of message about not trusting or missing support in your life. The key is to look at everything symbolically. Remember, what you are looking for are clues to how you are doing the same thing in your waking dream, how you are creating this hologram and consequently, how you can re-create it.

When a particular person appears in a dream, do not think literally that after 20 years this person is still plaguing you. If you have had no contact with them, have healed what was difficult between you both, you can know that they are appearing as an attribute which clearly represents something to you. Sometimes when someone in your present life shows up, it is harder to understand what they represent, because they may be many things to you now. Your soul will pass you the remembrance of someone who is a finished relationship, one you categorized as inferior, egotistical, limiting, abusive, or a number of different things. This way, when you are processing the information of the dream, you can have one word that describes this person to you now. Use that word to then dissect the rest of the dream.

For example, this person who shows up is really a fine person, but when you knew them, your final image of them was 'inadequate'. Now you are working with what I call your Lowest Self and that person represents your Lowest Self. Now observe the dream. What is that person or your own Lowest Self trying to do to you, and what is your reaction? Can you see how this process goes?

One of my clients related a dream she had the night before our session together. She felt it was very meaningful because it evoked such strong emotions, but she didn't know what it meant. She had a dream that a former boyfriend from years ago showed up just as she was about to have an out of body experience. She was lying on the bed, waiting for the spirit to rise (she had never done this in her waking dream) when this old lover showed up. He tried to stop her from continuing and told her she had better not go on because she was not ready. He tried to coax her and got in her way, and generally berated her about attempting such a dangerous thing. She sat up and started yelling at him that she no longer needed him in her life and this is what she wanted to do and she would do it. She became terribly angry with him and eventually lost the vibration to do the out of body experience. She woke up frustrated and didn't know why.

I asked her if she could find one word to describe how she felt about this old boyfriend, what would it be. She said she was not proud of it, but that word would be 'loser'. I then suggested that we follow this concept that he represented her Lower Self. By doing so, we could see the whole experience differently. Now, it was her own Lower Self trying to stop her from rising to a higher plane or have a metaphysical experience. She saw it as empowering instead of frustrating because she defended her desire and right to *rise above*.

The more you want to learn, the more there is for you. Every detail of the dream could represent something when seen through the language of symbolism. If you are in bed while dreaming, what does it mean to you? Is it a place where you truly rest, have positive loving experiences, feel cozy and loved, or is it a place of nightmares, ghosts and demons? If your dream takes place in a swamp, what does it mean? Is it a place filled with humidity and many forms of life, mystery, underwater possibilities, or feelings of sinking, lurking, and slowness? What fits for you is the point.

What about recurring dreams? Such dreams are just strong messages trying to come through about issues in your *waking* dream that you have chosen not to tackle. Once again, only the dreamer can interpret. What is the issue in the dream that is most disturbing or most lovely? Messages can come through as things that push and propel, create fear and discomfort, or things that compel and draw you towards something. Depending upon the nature of the dreamer, it is up to them to determine which message is most effective.

The point is, your dreams are manifestations of your combined conscious and unconscious mind and these manifestations represent your personal hologram. So why not understand the pattern through a third person similar to when you are watching a dream occur in your mind, and benefit from seeing the symbolism and learning from it? Can you do the same thing with the waking dream? I believe you can. The concept, once again, is seeing everything that happens as symbolic, representing some larger concept. Not only will you not take things so personally, but you can learn your lessons on the first or second try and not have to spin around endlessly repeating the same old pattern virtually forever.

Monsters and Angels

A concept I want to introduce here is about our deepest fears and our greatest longings. I believe that we, as group consciousness, create fear for a reason. It keeps us within the safety lines of the ego-created reality by creating something horrible outside this realm of protection, thus perpetuating the ego tribe/illusion. What those monsters represent is how vividly we can imagine and how deep our self-hate goes. I have discovered that humans all carry self-hate to some degree or another as part of the experience of the separation of the soul from our creator.

So monsters appear quite frequently in our society. They are not Loch Ness in nature, but they are humans like you, showing up as rapists, megalomaniacs, torturers, serial killers, bombers, terrorists, mass murderers, and whatever else creates the most fear and loathing deep in your heart. How do they fit into the dream you are dreaming? Who would include such a horrible nightmare and why?

I believe that these individuals themselves have identified with the archetype of the monster, the most evil one or dreaded fear itself because they believe that this archetype can be embodied. The ego creates archetypes, or patterns, that we relate to in some way. Some people carry the knight or hero archetype, which means they see themselves as either a chivalrous gentleman sort, caring for damsels in distress and protecting weaker ones, or as heroes, saving the underdog. Others carry the victim archetype, always being taken advantage of or somehow persecuted. Still others are the quintessential artist, vagabond, salesman, thief, adventurer or mother. You don't have to be one gender or another to embody any of these types. Given all these options and tons more, you will resonate with the one or ones closest to your temperament or predisposition. Carolyn Myss, in her book, *Sacred Contracts*, dedicates the book to archetypes and ways to find self-awareness and healing through understanding them. I suggest that the monster archetype represents the being that is the most loathsome for all of humanity. It is one character that no one likes, that everyone in every culture recognizes as bad or incarnate evil, or whatever you call it. Believe it or not, some people choose to embody that archetype. Remember, this manifest existence offers every possible choice for learning, growth, or simply for the choosing.

It's not a conscious choice. It is more a resonance, just like embodying any other archetype. Some time ago I was invited to a friend's house and while I was there noticed their 7-year-old son, Alexander, hiding. He didn't make himself known right away, but as soon as he joined us and I had a chance to talk to him, I could sense a very regal knight! He was such a little gentleman for 7 years old and carried himself with dignity and a mission. I asked what he liked to play with and he ran and got his Jedi Knight light sword. I mentioned to his parents that he carried the knight as his primary archetype, and they looked at each other and laughed. His father asked him to go and get his favorite toys. He quickly, and with much enthusiasm, ran and brought back a box of toy knights. I didn't know such things existed, and when I asked him which was his favorite he said, "The good knights, of course."

But there will be those who resonate with the bad knights as well, and with the archetype of monsters and heinous humans who do evil and unspeakable things. Why? (Remember, the question *why* only loops you around within the illusion). The best I can understand is that it is a place to resonate; it is at the very end band, and angels are at the other end. Sometimes one person can embody *both*. I'm always amazed when I hear about serial killers finally being caught and their neighbors say, "But he was such a great guy," or, "He was the perfect neighbor." This embodiment is a strange predisposition, but it exists; the being that embodies the very highest and the very lowest, all in the same incarnation.

These people represent for us what we all could become, the highest and the lowest, or our potential, as if someone had to hold those cards. The ones whose names are remembered throughout history as the most extreme cases of heinousness also remind us of our potential for self-hate. We all carry some amount of self-hate, but these monsters bring it to material form. Why? The answer is different for everyone who comes into contact with this type of abhorrent human expression. For some, it provides an opportunity to stretch the limits of forgiveness. For others who are more closely involved, it challenges them with personal lessons. However, those who resonate most exactly with this sort of vibration may call it into their lives, either through police investigation, personal loss and tragedy, or through someone intimately entangled in their life.

The strange thing is, it's almost as if someone must play that part to keep us all from stepping into it. I think we all have some of every possible potential residing within us. Some medical scientists believe we have the genetic knowledge of every living disease ever known to man, past and present and possibly future. It is already in us. We don't need to get sick to create the antibodies for each new strain of flu; we already have the code to create it. Do we all have the potential for every human attribute? Perhaps you sense the answer in the pit of your stomach. You don't want to admit it and your brain will not go along with it, but inside, you know you have been places you never dreamed you'd ever be and have done things you never expected to do in this life or another. Or rather, you believe you have done these things in your illusions, but they were simply that: illusions. You can wear any disguise you choose in your hologram, all to keep you from remembering who you truly are. It certainly provides another argument against judgment.

So what of society's monsters? Are they holding something at bay by manifesting this heinous trait, something so deep and dark that they seem destined to self-hate for centuries if they could remember what they did? And what of us, who read about them, who study them, who investigate them, are curious about them, repelled by them, attracted to them, angered by them? They are providing an opportunity for each person to have their own responses (that have nothing to do with the monster). Then the questions arise, "Why are we having our own specific responses? What are they lighting up in us? How can we see what we are made of by measuring ourselves against the greatest evil?"

Remember that changing responses helps you get off the hamster wheel. Does it mean you can come from forgiveness and love with everyone *except* this particular evil seed that the entire world loathes? No. Once again, you are challenged; in every case you are asked to come from forgiveness and love. If you cannot look at the most heinous situation that may have existed in your lifetime and say a prayer of peace and forgiveness for those who suffered, and the accused as well, you need to look at why you cannot.

Here's another reason for creating the *heinous* in your group hologram; they help you look at yourself in a group. Are you capable of mass genocide? Name one race or nationality that is not. Are you capable of torture and investigative procedures that bypass the limits of the law? Are you capable of killing and maiming without any guilt or remorse? Can you blow up thousands of living breathing human beings for some cause and not feel sad? We have engaged in these actions no matter what country we hail from and probably will continue to do so. Are we as a group capable of turning a blind eye to racist abuses and persecutions like the Klu Klux Klan? Are we as citizens of whatever country and whatever creed justified in killing, torturing and displacing millions of people for what we consider a greater good? Look at the Trail of Tears and the millions of Indians simply removed from their ancestral homes and sent to live in the most desolate places on the continent. We initiated those actions under the letter of the law and with threat of death.

Are you aware how your country extracts information from spies? Do you think it is pleasant? What about the Aztecs, a tribe of South American people we now think of as heroic and warlike, who simply slaughtered hundreds of native people each day in ritual ceremonies? They ripped the hearts out of their chests causing graphic torture and wrenching pain. Were we not there? What are we *really* not capable of doing?

So when you look at the heinous acts of a mass murderer, are you any different on some core level? Maybe you never actually lifted a hand to strip someone's skin off, but if you were alive as an American in 1945, you participated in the aftereffect of the destructive bombing of Hiroshima and Nagasaki that were as devastating and painful as having your skin ripped off. Now you are beginning to understand that the monster is our conscience made manifest, at least temporarily, originating from built-up group guilt. Then another aspect of our selves, our Highest Selves, arrives on the scene to light a path for us. We can throw rocks and become enraged and cry for the electric chair, but in there somewhere also is part of us. It is we who are asking for punishment, for our heinous behavior as a group, behavior that we have ignored, forgotten, not been told, or put out of our minds. To act out of anger, hatred, revenge, greed or righteousness is not something the ego ever lets us forget. The ego wants to use that information to keep us in self-hate forever, whereas the spirit uses the symbology of the serial killer, the mass murderer, the Satanist, or the megalomaniac to help us heal our own group wounds.

You can only be responsible for your own lessons, so looking at how you react is your first clue. Knowing that we/us/you put something horrible in our dream is the next clue. It is there for a reason. Ignore it, fight it, and it will persist again and again, for further learning and extensive tests. Embrace it for what it is, a part of you that has shown up on the radar screen that you most definitely don't want to see, but which needs desperately to be addressed and healed. And how do you heal? That depends on each person. What is the reaction, where will it lead you, what needs to be acknowledged in your own individual life?

Remember, it's your dream, and only you can interpret it. Only you can select another dream, but only after healing the previous dream. We are more connected than you realize, and to heal oneself is to heal a whole group. Bless the heinous, for they help us see who we might have become. They show us how to change the content of our dreams, and our holograms as well!

The Face of Innocence

In this illusion, we are aware of two faces: the face of good and the face of evil. From that simple discrimination, separation arises, and separation spawns judgment and judgment obliterates equality and equality goes with acceptance. Honesty and trust are then destroyed as humankind looks for ways to uphold differences and inequalities. As we have already discussed, separation is a tool of the ego world and is not known in the spirit realm. Simply realizing and observing this duality, however, is part of the voyage home. Identifying yourself as being a devil or an angel is not an acceptable stopping point in self-awareness.

Be aware that the face of innocence can be a trap when identified with sweetness versus badness. We believe there are those who do good, or they do more good than harm, at least. We associate healers, teachers, underpaid servants, candy stripers, nurses, volunteers, and hospice workers with good people. We think that bad should not happen to them. We think, especially if we are the innocent, that after all the good thoughts we have and good deeds we do and good things we produce, that we should not have to pay the bad tax. Why should bad things happen to us? Why doesn't the Red Sea part for us and for good reason? Why are we so discouraged when things don't go our way even though we spend so much time loving and giving and being a great person? In fact, it seems to be more devastating when we are thwarted or hurt in light of being such an angel.

This is another trap, that's all. We are still living the duality because we are still discriminating good versus bad. It doesn't matter what side of the fence you end up on in your own estimation, if it is one or the other, you are still trapped in the illusion.

What is duality and why is it important? Duality is the theory that two elements or modes are active in this reality; it is the belief that the universe operates under the influence of two opposing forces: good and evil. It is the belief that keeps judgment afloat. It says that it is not only correct to judge, it is wise to do so. It says that to know what is good and what is evil is considered safe by many. Most of the world feels that dualism is a truth, that the opposing forces are at work providing tension to this world. Why then is it important to understand duality, and not only understand, but to see beyond its limitations?

It is vitally important because duality is *not* a truth. It is part of the illusion, but it is not a truth in reality. Remember, I use the term *reality* to refer to what exists outside the illusion, or what is considered Truth. I once read an article by a woman who went into a diabetic shock, had a stroke, and was in a coma for several days. While she was in this coma, as the doctors called it, she was actually resting in a place that is not what we would call Earth. It was a place of such warmth and light that she could find no human words to effectively describe it. In her effort to try to convey this existence, or reality, she said these words:

> *Love is neither a noun or a verb. It is all there is. It is greater than energy, than Spirit, than God, than Universal Presence or any other definition you can think of.*

That sentence reverberated through my being as not only profound, but a truth. If love is indeed what reality is, how can separation exist, bringing with it judgment, feelings of failure, loneliness, loss, and inequity? Some things cannot co-exist, and divine love does not co-exist with separation.

What about choosing to identify with being sweet instead of evil? How can that be seen as a trap? It's because you are paying homage to duality. You have said, "Okay, I will choose. I choose innocence." Yet instead of choosing innocence over evil, you are actually choosing separation over love, because when you see yourself as sweeter, better, nicer or in any way *other* than someone else, you are investing in the belief that separation could be possible. Thus you throw your weight into the ring of the ego and not the spirit. Remember, you cannot choose both divine love and separation in *any* of its forms. So then, even though it appears you have chosen to be a good person, as long as you identify that you are only good in relation to someone who is bad, you have not chosen anything other than inequity, loss, failure, and loneliness.

Those who have chosen to express themselves through the archetype of the innocent are, in fact, deluding themselves even more than those who have chosen evil. Those who have chosen to express themselves in a dark or negative way do not think they are closer to God because of this exclusive choice. They feel the duality as strongly as others because they feel judgment, ostracism and loss of support. Of course, then, the innocents feel justified in judging and ostracizing them because our society condones it. Either way, we're playing the ego's game.

The only way out is to see beyond the limitations of inequality, to see beyond the body, to see beyond the disguise that anyone chooses to wear in this incarnation. But first, it is imperative to identify that choosing to express yourself as a sweet and loving person, unless you embody divine love, is exactly the same—*exactly the same*—as if you had chosen to express yourself as mean and spiteful. You have chosen a form of separation. What does that choice do to your righteous sense of judgment, to the pride you feel in being a good person, to the smugness you secretly conceal, but feel in the presence of those who openly do destructive or violent acts? Well, let's see, *pride, righteousness, smugness.* These emotions belong distinctly to the ego.

Let's picture another choice. What does choosing divine love look like? "Love is neither a noun or a verb, it is *all* there is." How would you describe that message? It would not include any judgment, but instead acceptance. It would not be acceptance out of your own goodness, but acceptance because where there is love, nothing else is possible other than complete acceptance of your brothers and sisters as being anything except what they are: Divine. You would not be able to put yourself on a higher rung of the ladder than another, nor would you be able to see someone on a higher or lower rung than you. The ladder does not and cannot exist. We are all equal.

The difference between choosing to be good, or wearing the mask of the good girl or good boy, and actually being Divine is that the first choice comes accessorized with judgment and the latter does not. It is that easy to ascertain. Either you behave as you do because it is consistent with your integrity and beliefs, which means you connect in a place of genuine love and therefore equality, or you behave as good people behave and in the back of your mind you judge others as either good like you or *not* good. The disguise is so well applauded you may not want to give it up, but it is a much subtler trap than you realize. Whatever archetype you relate to, or disguise you wear, acknowledge what it is: a disguise with an illusion. Once you have acknowledged it, you have taken one more step in retrieving power from the ego.

"A man is never more truthful than when he acknowledges himself a liar."

— Mark Twain

16 The Masquerade and the Mirror

We have spoken about the ego in many ways, alluded to its power, and seen how allocating power to it creates an insidious and sabotaging nature. It seems to continue camouflaging itself in ways to which we fall prey again and again. The following presents a way of perceiving that will remind you who and what you truly are.

There once was a grand masquerade ball, and you were invited to attend along with all the other royalty of your city. It was necessary, however, for each person attending to wear a costume so their true identity was not revealed. You gave some thought as to how you wanted to portray yourself. You might have gone to elaborate lengths to disguise your real self, or you might have chosen a costume to portray what you always wanted to be. Just imagine what the possibilities might have been. The object, remember, was to engage with others without giving away your true nature. You would then choose someone to dance with that fit your costume. Beauty needs her Beast, Cleopatra desires her Anthony, and Princesses require Princes. Clowns, jokers, harlequins, vampires, mummies, nurses, and kings would have been present, and no doubt you would have seen slick players, naïve schoolgirls, wolves in grannies' gowns, and innocents in red hoods. Also present were athletes, actresses, musicians, artists, salesmen, street people, and drunks. If you could imagine the costume, someone was wearing it. Some were so convincing that you wanted to gawk and point. Some acted out their costume persona so perfectly you might have wondered if that was not truly who they were. The dynamics of the ball created the ultimate outlet as each participant located those who not only were convinced they were who they presented themselves as (the wolf and red riding hood), but who completed their own picture (warlocks and witches). This scenario made the game so much fun that everyone could be who they either dreamed of being (a princess) or played out their alter ego (the street hooker) or vice versa. It also allowed you to get away with not taking responsibility for ethics or values or any future repercussions of what or who you truly were (for the duration of the party at least). No one knew who you were and could not hold you accountable. They were just responding to your grand elaborate costume as you were to theirs.

What if the party never ended? What if no one went home and became themselves again or the royalty never took their rightful place in the Kingdom? What if the costume provided a separate reality that became so engaging that no one remembered any other way? People might just forget who they really were. Is it possible that we could forget that we were wearing a grand elaborate costume? You would surely know it if you were wearing a Woman-in-Distress costume. Why would that guy wear a Stupid costume, always acting dumber than he is? And were they out of Princess outfits, or what? Why would anyone settle for Slightly Bulgy and Splotchy?

Let me suggest that the ball is a metaphor for actually what has happened to us. We are all wearing one costume or another as the manifestation of the ego. Some are quite nice, indeed, but they are all costumes. No one can see with the physical eyes who we really are, and especially not with such grand elaborate outfits distracting everyone so convincingly.

Each of us has chosen our own costumes. No one can choose a costume for someone else. It's just like Halloween costumes; you can't pick one out for someone else. It says something about your alter ego if you choose it yourself. It will differ from year to year depending upon the issues you are currently dealing with. One year I was discussing this idea with a group of students at a live-in school and one girl challenged my thesis indignantly. She said, "How can my costume have anything to say about me?" I asked her what her costume was going to be and she replied, "Dorothy from the Wizard of Oz." I laughed out loud. How obvious, I thought. "You just want to go home, don't you?" I suggested, and with that she broke down crying and left the room. I guess it may have said more about her than she was aware of herself. The same goes with the ego costume, except it has been chosen unconsciously, before you even remember being invited to the masquerade ball.

So now what is this whole dance about; flirting and mingling with people that we actually may not know at all? We may think we are engaging with the genuine article, but in fact, we are simply left with a glass slipper at the end of the night.

Let's look at some current costumes. If you think symbolically, you have already placed people you know into those outfits I used as examples earlier. Now let's look at regular everyday people. What are their costumes? What is the benefit they derive from them? A common one is the Fool. It's an easy costume to put together, and no one asks anything of you. They have no expectations, and no disappointments, right? You're off the hook to your Highest Self. Another costume I often encounter is the Nurse. This one allows the wearer to put others' concern and safety first, gives them a viable and worthwhile task to do, and allows them to feel better about themselves as they constantly exhibit selfless behavior. It helps them build self-worth, but they're not allowed to pamper their *own* selves. Other costumes may include the Invalid, the Pauper, the Cynic, the Martyr. We must not forget the Knight. Guess who he finds to dance with? Could it be a Helpless Maiden? You're catching on. What happens when the helpless maiden finds independence? Do you have the courage to change costumes?

Does this discussion suggest that we are all acting? Does anyone really know who anyone is? Are we all playing in some drama we know nothing of, consciously? If the answer is yes that means that who you *are* may have nothing whatsoever to do with the costume you are wearing. However, everything you *believe* you are is all about the costume, and that fact creates a serious dichotomy. Something inside you knows you are more than the costume, but you have worn it so long you cannot remember who you were before you put it on, or even why you put it on. Perhaps only a seed remains of your true nature, but a memory of it still exists somewhere.

Let's look at the intricacies of your ego-created masquerade ball. Not only do you wear a single costume, I find that you have many. Some costumes are worn only for specific relationships, maybe to change the dynamic to more power or less responsibility. Would it be convenient to wear the Helpless or Mentally Distressed costume in certain relationships? Do you wear the Unlovable outfit when you are involved with someone who is wearing their Unable to Love garb? That way you can't blame the other for what does not transpire and you're not disappointed. The reasons for choosing the costumes are as complex as you care to see, and also as insane. Do not look for sense or sanity. You will only find illusions and egoic images.

The difficulty in trying to find your true identity is that everything, and I literally mean *everything,* in this material world will uphold your masqueraded self, and that truth is because of the Mirror. The Mirror is essentially everything in which you see yourself reflected. It is not simply a physical mirror, but it is the eyes of those who look upon you. It is the responses you receive from others and yourself according to your behavior (in playing the role of the costume). It is consensus agreement, mass consciousness, and the shared belief that the masquerade ball is the *real* world. It all becomes clear when you use your physical eyes and they reflect the ball everywhere you look, and nothing else exists. It is only when you begin to see *through* the ball that things get really confusing and your very foundation no longer feels stable. If this book appeals to you and you recognize its premise, then you have seen through the shallowness and transparency of the ego world at one point or another along your spiritual journey or you have felt it's lack of quality as you require more authenticity.

Let's look at the Mirror. Often times when you ask the question, "Who am I?" you go to the mirror and stand in front of it believing that what is reflected back is the answer. This gives you the only answer the ego-created world wants you to see. You become weary of the outdated and sorry outfit you have worn for such a long time. You try to update the outfit by having it cleaned, or you opt for a completely new wardrobe as you change careers, acquire new partners, go on health kicks or cleanses of various types, or move to a different place and take on a new persona. These actions are all more of the same, just variations on a theme of playing a role. Nonetheless, you still keep looking in the mirror to find your identity, whether it is a physical mirror or the reflection the tabloids and glamour magazines give you.

If you go to a gym, you will most likely see mirrors all around the room. They are present to help the participants see themselves and make sure they are doing their exercises properly. These mirrors surrounding you become a metaphor for the ego world. Are you doing everything properly and evenly? Do you look good enough? Can you see those around you without actually engaging? You can see them through the mirror also, so you know they are there, but you don't have to look them in the eyes and find a place of deeper connection. Everyone is upholding the image of the Mirror. Mirror, mirror, on the wall, who's the fairest of them all? The Mirror will tell.

When you get dressed in the morning to face the world, what is the first thing you do? You get up and go look in the bathroom mirror to scrutinize the face, the pores, the facial hair, the bloodshot eyes, the bags, the wrinkles, and you find the blemishes. Even before you brush your teeth, you must catch the whole picture of what you are brushing for. You want white teeth that represent health and vitality, but mostly you're looking for beauty. Is that who you are? Where is the part that lives forever, that never gets old, and never gets hurt? Where is the part of you that moves on after your physical bag of bones and wrinkles have become lifeless? Do you ever see that part of you in the Mirror? No, the Mirror knows nothing of that. It only reflects Ego. Like a vampire in a mirror, the Spirit Self is not reflected there.

When you look for assistance in finding your true nature, what do you get? Counseling or religious advice all seems to come with a list of judgments about all the things you are doing wrong or right that you need to start or stop doing. It's just more of the actor acting out the costume. Some people choose to critique and analyze the ball, some try to understand the mechanisms that create the machinations, and others will make their whole journey in this incarnation a study of bringing logic and sense into the masquerade ball. That process is part of their personal understanding that one day brings them to Truth. But do not let their perceptions influence your own search. Within the illusion, no one's truths are any more correct than another's.

Finding the True Nature under the Costume

Where can you find the True Nature? Do not look in the Mirror to find it. Do not look to others as they will only see what you present to them, which remember, is your costume. They are showing you their costumer as well. In fact, can you honestly say how many people you have genuinely connected with in the past length of time? Are you buying their bit-part acting job as much as they are investing in yours? Who is that person behind the mask? How many people, if any, can you say really know you? Even those you love the most are convincingly astute at staying true to their acting character. However, as you listen to them day in and day out, your logical brain asks how can this costume not be true character? How can they not be what they convince you they are? They have convinced themselves so how could you not be swayed? But again and again, the only truth to be found in this illusion is through the doorway of love.

Within the illusion, every problem that presents itself can only be solved through love. Love and thoughts of love are the only things that are eternal, the only things that shine through the illusion and speak of Truth. No matter what you are up against, no matter how horrible, how full of suffering or depression your situation seems, your only eternal exit (as in stepping off the wheel) is in choosing love. You must see through the illusion to learn who or what you are dealing with. If your problem includes a boss or a husband, engaging with the actor is a lesson in immeasurable repetition. If it involves a mother or child, confronting and connecting with the ego façade only results in frustration and capitulation. Again and again, no matter how heavy the situation seems to be, it is just another scene in the ego play. Pulling back the curtains and seeing the True Nature is what is now required. You have learned all you can by interfacing with the actors. Your next step is unveiling Truth.

Who are you then? Who is behind the mask? Who are any of us? Remember that I said the ones who attended the first masquerade ball were royalty? Clue One is you are indeed royalty, only not of the elite and exclusionary variety. You are Divine royalty. We were *all* created by the Original Creator of Life, Love, and the Universe. You are divine, inspired love energy.

Clue Two, all the things you have done under the guise of your costume, you have not been responsible for. How could that be true? Consensus reality says you must pay for all your sins, your government even says you must pay extra taxes for sins (tobacco and liquor), but your true nature knows nothing of these *sins* done in your costumed self. Remember, I am referring to your *true* Self, not your egoic self, which would have you believe you are heinous. Sins and guilt were created as part of the masquerade ball world; they are not part of reality, which came before the ball. All the results of sin and guilt belong clearly in the realm of its creator, in this case, *inside* the illusion. So get used to it, you are *sinless*! The authentic, divine self of everyone who exists is sinless.

You may recall that the whole object of the ball was to obscure everyone's true identity from one another. This is Clue Three. Obscuring identity is the nature of the ego world. If the ego's definition is all you seek, keep your eye firmly on the Mirror, for that image is what it will uphold. If you seek more, it is time to see through the Mirror.

Years ago on my husband's birthday, I spent an elaborate evening dressed up as a woman I was not (blonde curly wig, fake breasts, sexy clothes borrowed from various friends, someone else's perfume, and even a slightly chipped-looking tooth). I took the bus into San Francisco from the North Bay straight into the Mission District where he worked, which was also a pretty unsafe area at night. I was banking on the idea that he would recognize me fairly soon and give me a lift back home. I wanted to do something creative and fun, and hoped it would evolve into a romantic and interesting evening. I thought it would be a great memory maker! What happened was memorable indeed, but not the way I anticipated. First of all, my makeup was so convincing that my husband did not even recognize me and refused to give me a ride home. I had to beg and plead and bring up names of the students I had heard him talk about so he would not leave me stranded in the Mission at 10:00 at night. Finally, he conceded to give me a ride, but it was anything but romantic. He seemed annoyed and just wanted to get home. Little did he know that what he wanted to get home to was right beside him in the car. I made some small talk and he still did not know it was me. I started feeling a little panicky. I hadn't anticipated that outcome. As we drove along Van Ness Avenue I had the most horrible feeling in the pit of my stomach. Here was this person I knew and had grown to love, a person who knew me better than any living soul, and he did not *know* me. He looked in my eyes and saw someone else. That moment could never be reproduced, and I will never forget the hollowness and empty feeling of being invisible to someone I loved. The grand ball is just the same. The very purest nature of our divine essence is completely invisible to those who apparently love us the most, and most of the time to ourselves as well. So then, who knows that this grand, pure nature exists?

I have worked with clients in healing sessions for years and found that even those who believe that they are evil beings will admit that they know that something exists deep inside them that is more. Even though nothing in the Mirror shows us, we all seem to feel that somewhere in our heart of hearts or deepest suspicions, something higher is present. Even if it simply comes in a thread of knowing that we were meant to do something bigger than what we presently do, it is there. Throughout our sessions, clients may feel any number of emotions and feelings, depending upon what we uncover; but invariably the tears flow when we locate the divine essence and I describe to my client that I am connecting to a radiant divine being of intense love and magnitude. They are prepared to locate evilness and a loathsome nature, but when we encounter divinity, nothing can harden them to the response of vulnerability and honesty. I am never met by looks of doubt or questioning, only a great sense of relief that someone finally has greeted the real thing.

Because of the nature of my work, connecting to the Highest Self of all my clients, it has never been a question as to whether the soul of someone is divine or evil. That is a knowing that comes from touching again and again the very highest, purest self and seeing its dignity and wisdom. Those who have never had such experiences derive beliefs about the core of human nature from the acts of the masqueraders. It seems logical to make such an assessment given one's deeds as testimony of the person. Man *must* be evil to be capable of such acts of inhumanity we've witnessed not only in our century, but throughout history as well. The actor that masquerades as your genuine nature is capable of anything that can be thought, but it still doesn't reveal who you *are*. Is a soul simply the compilation of one's thoughts? What is it that continues to exist after the brain has become inactive and the blood stops carrying oxygen to it? What continues is the essence or life force energy, and who can ascribe negative or positive traits to pure energy? Energy may have been used to generate some negative deeds, thus leaving behind a trail of darkness or discomfort, but the pure energy used to make something come to life is just that: pure energy.

> *Within the dream of bodies and of death is yet one theme of truth, no more, perhaps, than just a tiny spark, a space of light created in the dark, where God still shines. – A Course in Miracles*

To look at the acts of a person and judge them accordingly is to not understand *who they are*. Our ego selves have done heinous and despicable deeds at some point on our journey, but that does not make us heinous and despicable; it only makes us ones who have *experienced* heinous and despicable things.

Let me reiterate, if you expect to see parts of your divine nature reflected back to you from others, it rarely happens. As I've described above, others will see you through your acts or words. Whatever you show them through the mask is what they will see and ultimately respond to. You cannot come up to someone while wearing a wolf's suit and say, "Hi, honey, what's cookin'?" without creating a bit of apprehension and fear, *even* if you are a sheep under it. You may know you wouldn't harm a flea, but the one seeing you does not know this, not unless they see around the costume. Occasionally we all see through the costume, and those rare glimpses are invaluable. Those moments, when someone lets their front down and admits something, or you witness something tender when they are not aware anyone is watching, can hold together a relationship long after logic says to give it up. In these moments, you *know* that something else is there *and* you know it is precious.

By examining responses and behaviors, we all have learned to judge, to choose and to love each other. If someone is kind to you, you like them. If someone is rude to you, you avoid them. If someone is antagonistic towards you, you prepare to defend yourself when you are around them. We all react to the big masquerade game. Didn't your mother ever tell you that the ones who picked on you the most were the ones who really liked you the most? Didn't you ever figure out that the ones who avoided you like the plague had the biggest crush on you? Didn't you ever realize in high school that the ones who made fun of you might very well be the ones who were, in fact, actually jealous of you? Haven't you figured out that the ones with the hardest exterior have the softest center? With communication like this, is it any wonder that the world is at war and no one can get along? So since you would admit that what you see is often not what you get, maybe there is something other than what you see with your eyes.

Keep in mind that if someone is responding to your costume, you most likely are responding to theirs. And as you respond with guilt, fear, or defensiveness, you are simply responding to someone's acting skills with egoic emotional choices. Take an example of a person you are involved with, either at home or work, who is controlling, and they take their job of managing the world seriously. Let's call them Moses. They expect you to follow them into the wilderness for 40 years if it is needed (as determined by them). You don't do well in the desert wilderness; some people don't have a tolerance for heat, but Moses doesn't care. It comes down to wills colliding. Now let's look behind the screen. Moses is a divine soul exactly like you. Why should you go into the wilderness because his divine soul says to go? No reason, unless you believe the actor who is playing Moses and are convinced that he knows something you don't. He may have talked to God, but you *are* God, remember? So taking this relationship one step past the lesson of 'relationships as tools for healing the self', you see *we are all the same.* That's right, we are equal and sinless and divine! You've learned your lesson. You have grown and healed. Now what? This is now what. You see beyond the mask that created your particular dynamic. Doing so not only ceases the challenging dynamic, or should I say, it ceases the emotional reaction to that dynamic, it guides you both Home. Remember that the purpose of this book is to assist you find your way Home, to return to where you came from, or rather, simply to *remember* it.

As *A Course in Miracles* says,

> *Where God is, there are you. Such is the truth. Nothing can change the knowledge given you by God into unknowingness. Everything God created knows its Creator.*

"As opposed to feeling the frustration about not knowing how to wake up, accept my truth when I tell you that you are already Awake."

— Dialogue on Awakening

17   The Fear of Awakening

One day while walking in the forest, I was bothered by a dream I'd had the night before. It was haunting me, because it was very unsettling. I dreamed about a foreboding character of doom, similar to something you'd see in a creepy horror movie, and once it showed up in your life, it was too late. Everything you ever knew would disintegrate, or disappear as if it had never existed. I woke up in fright as the black caped, ghostly demon approached the end of my bed. All I could see were the eyes, like bright beady lights, and all else was just a feeling of doom and coldness. From the pit of my stomach I had no doubt that everything I knew would be gone almost as soon as I recognized this being: my life, my husband, my property, my belongings, even my soul, all that was mine or that was me, poof, gone. Sensing my anxiety, my husband woke me up, assuring me that nothing was there. However, as I tried to go back to sleep, I wondered about the symbolism of the character and what was behind that fear. As I drifted off, I could hear my own voice say, "It is the fear of Awakening," but I let it go, unready or unwilling to deal with that thought.

Later as I was hiking down a wooded trail, I asked for a confirmation that the dream was indeed warning me that I had come face to face with my own fear of awakening, though I really had no doubt. Then, I voiced my fear out loud, "I have a fear of Awakening." Just at that moment, I struck my head rather fiercely on a fallen tree. I had to laugh out loud. It was a message with a swift blow to the head!

Coming to terms with the knowing that you are greater, more powerful, and more brilliant than you ever imagined is going to light up some things. It is definitely going to rock the ego boat. Any number of things could occur, from creating a change in every relationship you are in, to sending you into a void-like depression. When changes occur in the core of who you believe you are, every other belief built on that belief is altered. It is similar to remodeling a house while still trying to live in it. Your spirit is trying to guide you to your own awakening and the ego is desperate to keep that from happening.

A Course in Miracles says,

> You **will** undertake a journey because you are not at home in this world. And you **will** search for your home whether you know where it is or not. If you believe it is outside yourself the search will be futile, for you will be seeking it where it is not. You do not know how to look within yourself for you do not believe your home is there.

The Course further states that by guiding your brothers or your fellow beings home, you are essentially following the Voice for God. Seeing through the illusory masks to their true selves is how you guide them.

Einstein created a hypothetical situation in which he pictures physicists inside an elevator falling from its cables in the shaft of a very tall building. These men are performing experiments, in perfect isolation from the world outside the elevator, to ascertain what is happening to them. They remove objects from their pockets and release them. Nothing happens to these objects. They don't drop to the floor because they are falling at exactly the same rate as the men and the elevator. If the scientists jump into the air or propel the objects, they float within the elevator at the same proportional velocity with which they were propelled. Given their perspective, tools, and experiences, the physicists are naturally led to believe that they are free from gravity, perhaps suspended in outer space, even though they are falling disastrously to their deaths. Einstein then supposes that this elevator of scientists is actually transported into outer space and suspended by a cable, free from gravity. They are asked to determine if their elevator is being pulled up, lowered down, or even swinging around in circular motion experiencing centrifugal force. Here is the point: these brilliant physicists would not be able to ascertain the answer for themselves (using their tools and experiences *within* the box). Even more extraordinary, assuming they were actually being swung around in circular motion, they would firmly believe that the floor on which they were standing was *down*, even though down has no meaning in such a situation. They have no way to determine *reality* from *within* the box.

The *Course* suggests that we also cannot see outside the dream. We need someone on the outside, or someone awake, who can tell us where the door is, how to awaken, what is really going on, and what distortions have arisen from being in the elevator so long. We don't know what is up or down. Some of those in the Earth Illusion have awakened, and calling upon their wisdom for assistance is not only a great idea, apparently it is critical. Whether you find a relationship with Christ, Mohammad, Krishna, Buddha, or other Ascended Masters, I stress the importance of finding some association as you begin to awaken.

Once you acknowledge that you are not who you believe you are, and you begin to see through the illusion that masks your Highest Self, what can you expect?

You can expect to be met with your own fear of awakening. Remember, it is only fear that prevents you from being one with your True Nature, with your Creator in eternal peace. Behind every resolution of one fear, another variation of fear resides. How do you dissolve the fear before you know what awakening is actually like?

Do you remember getting ready to go to high school or college? You were scared. You didn't know where any of the classrooms were, where your locker was going to be, or who your teachers were. You were afraid of being humiliated, late, embarrassed, lost and alone. Then you went to orientation where you met some of your teachers, received a map of the whole campus, and located your locker. You pored over the map, memorized the room number of every classroom, highlighted the numbers in yellow, and discovered you were no longer afraid. You just have to find your equivalent of that orientation to Awakening.

Mental Scrapbooking

Do you remember the photo album of memorable events in your mind's eye that I mentioned earlier? If you are having a really joyful experience, you're totally absorbed, and you want to remember it forever, consciously earmark the event and store it in this mental album. Originally, I earmarked mine so that when I die, I would have preselected the memories I want to pass through again.

My first earmarked moment was years ago when I lived aboard a sailboat. It was a cold Sunday morning and I was sitting on the couch, ceramic heater pulled up to my legs, and I was savoring a piece of my mother's homemade Hauska, a sweet bread she makes at Christmas. I had just taken it from the toaster and buttered it; the smell and the taste, coupled with the feeling of snugness and warmth in my fuzzy slippers, was overwhelming. I vowed I wanted to remember this feeling forever, and I did. It is still there along with many other delicious and delightful moments in my mental scrapbook.

Earmarking memorable moments can be your Orientation, and will contain everything you need. If you experience what it will be like to know you are Awake, then you not only will lose your fear, but you will be moving yourself closer and closer towards this awareness each time you place yourself in those moments. What is it that these moments all have in common that provides the necessary feeling or energy of awakening? They all contain *joy*. The only other commonality is that you are totally *present* in each situation. The memorable moments you earmark won't contain distracted thinking about many other things, nor will they occur when you are worrying, having anxiety, or are in a state of mental confusion or chaos. You will just simply be there, enjoying the moment for the unique, however mundane, experience that may never come again in exactly that configuration. Think of one example right now. Pull up a fond memory that brings a smile to your face. Now, as you recall it, and then, as you lived it, you experience joy and presence.

Joy plus *Presence* equals *Peace*. That's it. It isn't reliving the events, as much as it is the feelings they all hold for you. Memorable moments of joy all contain a bit of the peace of God, which is all that Awakening is.

I started flipping through my entire mental album. Right on the first page was my mother's toasted and buttered Hauska, along with memories of my husband laughing either at something I had said that caught him off guard, or of me laughing at him as he fell into some caricature or another. Sometimes my seams felt like they would bust. My album also displayed memories of sitting in a café with my dear friend drinking chai. I can remember the window seat we had, how we had watched the pedestrians, and how we had spoken so passionately about religion, love, spirit and expectations. I never wanted the moment to end. We were connected, with minds alike, happy to be together like young girls, giggling and touching hands. *Joy* plus *Presence* equals *Peace*. I thought I was going to have to find a rocking chair for my porch and learn how to knit before I could ever find peace. But I can do joy! I live for joy. The presence part is a little more challenging, but it just requires remembering or reminding.

You don't have to develop cancer to realize your life is already speckled with joy. Stopping to notice it and deciding to be present is what brings the peace that then reminds you of your Home. Reminding you of your Home is what decreases the fear of awakening that lurks in your dreams, and it is what keeps you constantly preoccupied. *Joy* plus *Presence* equals *Peace*.

One thing that I notice, as I try to bring my mind into present tense again and again as it wanders off into the past or future, is that I feel some anxiety. While pondering this occurrence, the message I received was that the mind is being forced out of its comfort zone, out of a natural and recurring pattern. It has not found comfort in this new process of being present yet. It is neither good nor bad; it is simply an understanding of why you may feel anxiety as you try to stay in present tense. If you allow yourself to return to a past judgment or to become involved in solving a future problem, your anxiety will cease because that is the pattern the brain is familiar with. However, if you continue into uncharted territory, in peace and presence, you will feel anxiety or discomfort until eventually the mind will come to see this presence as normal.

So the key becomes to *make* as many of these memorable moments now as you can. That way you don't have to go looking into the past for help. Look squarely into the now for your Orientation and the more you live in joy and presence, the more the groggy dream of illusion begins to fade. As you face your fears in whatever form they appear, remember it is assured that we all will Awaken for two reasons. One is that everything seeks its true nature, and two, it is God's will that we awaken and God's will then is already done.

Joy plus *Presence* equals *Peace*.

"Hallucinations disappear when they are recognized for what they are. This is the healing and the remedy. Believe them not and they are gone. All you need to do is recognize you did this. Once you accept this simple fact, and take unto yourself the power you gave them, you are released from them."

– A Course in Miracles

18 Lifting the Veil

There are many ways to find the key to your awakening, but no matter which key you use, you will eventually open a door that greets God. When that happens, it will forever change the way you see this world and yourself.

In a conversation with a dear friend of mine who is a poet, she was telling me about having some of her poetry critiqued. The conversation became more intense as she related to me what this editor had told her after reading her poems. Several of my friend's works were presented in the third person and were about very personal issues of abuse or death. Her editor and teacher looked her straight in the eye and said, "These experiences are yours, aren't they?" My friend could only nod. The editor continued by saying, "You are creating a veil between you and your reader. You're not fooling anybody. We know it is you, so *lift the veil.*" As my friend said this, we both stopped speaking and realized that we had stumbled upon a truth. We then realized why she writes poetry and why I paint. We want to know who we really are! It's what drives people to create, to express themselves in artistic or symbolic ways. We seek representations to help us re-create a way to see where the veil is. We are all looking for a way to lift the veil, because it is the barrier that stands between us and our most vulnerable, precious selves.

Lifting the veil so important because what is on the other side of the veil is your godliness. Why must you protect it? Why can't you just put it on display? Why do you feel so vulnerable when you expose that part of you? Why are you a nervous wreck when you put your creative product on display for others to see? Why do you create a wall around your heart so others cannot poke around uninvited? What are you most afraid of? Why is lifting the veil maybe the hardest thing you could ever do? The answer is jarring and profound. If you actually lift the veil and look eye to eye with your own godliness, the light would blind you.

You may wonder how to lift the veil without blinding yourself. Essentially this whole book has been about finding the path to your own godliness, so to give you directions in two easy steps would be unfair.

However, one thing is certain, in all your activities things will happen that provide the opportunity to lift the veil. Whether it is through a maturing and intimate relationship, probing deeper into your heart of hearts or a through a creative project whose authenticity calls for exposing what you are about, you will constantly create experiences that allow you to come face to face with God. The hardest part of coming face to face with God is when you see it, you will recognize it has been *You* all along.

Had our poet friend written in the first person, it would have brought the reader closer to the topic and created a sense of intimacy that speaking in the third person lacked. It was the difference in being a participant and being an observer. Who is having the actual experience, and who do you want to learn from? You trust someone who has walked a mile in your shoes. The observer can only surmise who it is, but does not know experientially. This knowledge differentiates between one who is awakening and one who is asleep. One knows who he is, the other can only take someone's word for it. Yet we all know at some level, and we can never lose all memory of our godliness.

When you encounter a situation where you feel dreadfully uncomfortable and overly emotional, perhaps you are being given a chance to open the door to your own godliness; and the closer you get to it, the more discomfort arises, because you have padded this vulnerable, precious inner self with a wall of profanity. You have insisted that you are not God, and so you have pasted all sorts of images of yourself as evil or worthless or inferior around its home. That way, whenever it might try to glimpse an image of itself, it will only see failure. The only problem with this heinous attempt to sabotage your own God-Self is that you did not create this godliness. That means that you do not have the code to amend it, ever. No matter what you may think of yourself or how you might try to trash or destroy yourself, you cannot change the nature of your Divine Self. You do not have that power. You can think whatever you want about yourself, or others for that matter. You can be convinced beyond a shadow of a doubt that you or someone you know is a product of the devil, born from evil, producing only chaos and destruction, and it will not matter one iota. *Nothing you can do will ever change the nature of who you truly are.*

As you read the following message, listen to what it is saying about you; it is who you genuinely are. I know because I too have experienced it.

> *You are infinitely loving; you are eternally peaceful,*
> *kind, gentle, caring, open, accepting, genuine, calm,*
> *generous, affectionate, warm, nurturing. You are so*
> *loving and peaceful that even as I recall those Divine*

*Beings that I have experienced, I cannot help but
be calmed simply by the remembrance of them. The
overwhelming presence of peace and contentment
is awe-inspiring. It is a feeling of no need, of deep
contentment and fulfillment, as if the act of loving
were all there is to joy.*

I know this because I have experienced it again and again and
each person I see, even though they may have unique attributes
of childlikeness or deep wisdom, there is a commonality of love
and peace beyond measure.

Once while I was working, I had the impression that the
physical body of my client was flickering like a video signal. I
quickly put that thought out of my mind, knowing that I would
never be the same if I believed that was possible. I continued
my work only to witness it again, and I knew what this meant.
I knew that the being I was connecting with, emitting genuine
love and peace, was actually the *real* article, and the physical
body was the hologram, not the other way around. I may have
believed this previously with my mind, but to experience it
made it unshakeable. No one can remove a truth once you have
accepted it as yours, and I knew as I know anything, that I was
encountering a truth. I knew that the being I was seeing, who
was emanating infinite love and eternal peace, was and is *who we
are.* It is how we were created.

I can feel the essence of which one is the enduring one. I
could also see the flicker of the body and realized that when it is
extinguished, it won't change one single particle of the original
blueprint. This physical person who most people would wager
is real, was actually the *hologram,* and the spirit, which we think
of as ephemeral and wispy, unconfined by walls or limitations of
time and space, was actually *real.*

The symbolism of the heart is all about mercy, love and a
deeper knowing, and these attributes are the closest you can

come to the authentic you. We are infinitely loving and eternally peaceful. Then the closer you can come to peace and love in this physical reality, the closer you are to experiencing your authentic godliness. This protection you try so hard to maintain is actually just protecting some costume jewelry, and the crown gems are elsewhere. No wonder we all feel like fakes; no wonder we don't want to expose our most authentic selves; no wonder we hide our innermost hearts from criticism. We are simply being fooled by a magician, another analogy for the ego self. We actually *are* parading as something we are not, unless we are exposing our most divine natures.

When you lift the veil, turn around and face your godliness. Do not be fooled by your misperceptions and manifestations of untrue thinking. Expose your Divine Self, and then start handing out sunglasses, because it's going to get bright! In every situation, make a conscious choice to respond in peace, or to remain in peace, and watch as your world begins to readjust itself to your Divine Self. When you are asked to allow admittance into your heart of hearts, usher them in gladly, not through the house of distorted mirrors, but directly into the place where your greatest love and peace reside. Remember, nothing you can believe can limit who you actually are, so take a leap of faith and open the real door.

Understanding the Divine Blueprint

If you had a glass of water and you firmly believed that it was *you*, that belief would determine many things about that glass and what to do with it. You might decorate the glass. You might move it to different locations, throw it down in anger, offer it to others, or water your plants with it. Your awareness would be centered on your glass of water, and much of your time and effort would be expended in protecting this single glass of water. Let's use this analogy to help understand the Divine Blueprint.

Let's say that the glass is your physical body and the water is your Christ Consciousness or Divine Self.

What happens to water? It may evaporate and return to the moisture in the sky where it becomes part of a cloud that rains back onto the earth. Then it either returns to the underground to become part of the aquifer, or it falls into the sea that circles the planet, bringing life to physical beings and replenishing the earth. You can spill water out of your glass or channel it in different directions; it can take different forms, but the water itself won't be destroyed. It can move through limitations we view as solid, such as earth. It can float through the air against gravity. It can become invisible to our physical eyes, and transform overnight from an unsupportable substance to one that can hold the weight of ice skaters, ice fishers, and large tractors.

Water can express itself as steam, fog, ice, snow, or crystals, but its nature will still be water. When you try to capture water and put it in a glass, you have not changed the nature of that water, but you now perceive that the water is either more special or less. It is more pure or more contaminated. The glass is more full or less full, and it certainly is separate from the rest of the water in the universe. Is it possible that all water contains the same chemistry? Allowing for unique variations of minerals and other chemicals appearing *in* water, the base that is water stays essentially unchanged.

Water is the universal solvent. It changes things from being stuck to being unstuck (remember the burnt pan soaking for 2 days in water?). It changes the effects of gravity if bodies are in it. It can destroy thousands of little glasses if they are lined along the beach during a tsunami wave. Water expresses itself in hurricanes, floods, gentle rains, thunderclouds, underground rivers, oceans and a drop of dew, but the essence is unchanged. All water comprises two parts hydrogen and one part oxygen (H_2O).

Water is life itself to all who live in the ocean. It brings revitalization to crops, skin, terrain, vegetation, and organs. It can turn a dried up useless object into a full and life-giving being. Without water, no life as we know it would exist on this planet.

Think about the awesome power of water as an analogy to the spirit. Have you ever witnessed a house sliding down a hill simply from so much rain that it washed the earth right out from under it? Have you ever been in the ocean and felt it toss around a steel boat like it were a rubber duck in a bathtub? Have you seen footage of an oil tanker being snapped in two by a breaking wave? Perhaps you've witnessed the amazing power of a whirlpool though it employs just a single spiral. No doubt you've experienced the overwhelming power and potential energy of a thunderhead, which, when harnessed, could supply electricity to millions. Have you ever flown through a cloud, which looked innocent enough in its etheric quality of no substance, only to be thrown around like you were in a pile of falling boulders? Water, in one form or another, has the power to destroy all of existence, yet it can express itself with delicacy and beauty. Think of a single snowflake sitting gently on a dark glove. Have you ever been more awed at the intricacy and delicacy of this tiny, temporary expression of water? Its beauty is beyond words. Watching the morning sun on dewdrops is one of life's more peaceful moments. As you cool off in a clear stream on an August day, you experience yet another quite different expression of water just was you do when you take a hot shower after being in the freezing rain.

Water also displays the properties of distortion (refraction) and reflection. If you see a pencil inside a glass of water, you will witness a distortion as you see it become jagged where it comes out of the water, even though you know the pencil is straight. Is this phenomenon a way to show us that just because we see it with our physical eyes does not mean it is *real*? The reflection in a puddle, a lake, or even on a wet road or surface is a metaphor that allows us to see something in another way, upside down perhaps.

Water is all healing, life giving, and beautiful. It can be calm. It can be fierce. It can be used to clean, to baptize, and to refresh. It can be many things.

Now, to think that you can capture the nature of water in your little glass and make it special is to completely misunderstand the multiplicity of water's essence. This multiplicity brings us around to our Christ Consciousness or Divine Blueprint. Imagine that the H^2O of water is the blueprint that is actually you. It can express itself in many forms. Things can be put in it and it can be put in things that are contaminated, but the essence will always remain unchanged. This truth is the nature of our True Selves, our water selves, our Divine Blueprint. Your spirit was created by the Great Creator, which means the essence of you is pure creation energy. As we have already discussed, by the very nature of something being creation energy, it cannot *keep* itself from extending creation energy. Creation energy creates and extends its energy to everything it creates. Whether you feel deserving or valuable enough to receive creation energy from the Great Creator, you already have. In fact, you cannot *help* but have received this energy. As with the water analogy, it isn't your choice. If you are created water, you have all the properties available to you that water has. Your spirit is infinitely creative and all powerful.

Imagine, then, this glass or body you use to limit and define yourself. Can you see how ludicrous it now feels to limit all the potential of timelessness and space and matter by holding on to the image that you are simply one glass of water? Maybe yours is a tall iced tea glass, or a huge beer stein, or a shot glass; however, in light of what you are in essence, they are embarrassingly miniscule.

Perhaps the concept of us all being One makes more sense now. Take everyone out of their glasses, or bodies, and you will find the same essence or Oneness of Being. That Oneness cannot be separated, even though we believe it can. If it is hot and dry out, regardless of whether your glass is small or tall, the water will evaporate eventually. It is the same with people. If we are constantly being bombarded with negative experiences and emotions, we will all begin to suffer as a whole.

When I spoke in the last section about who you really are, I was referring to this massive, all-powerful, and all pervasive water aspect. Now let me describe it again. It is your Christ Consciousness, which means you are the expression of God. Remember, God is Love, so guess what that makes you? You cannot even imagine how loving it makes you. Yet, though you might not be able to imagine, you *do* know. No one has forgotten they belong to the Order of Godliness, even though the glass may have no awareness of it at all. For example, let's say you live in a desert and you have this glass of water; you shade it, protect it, and nourish it. This water has never seen other glasses of water or maybe even a thunderstorm, but it still carries the memory that it is more. That is the same as those who have not consciously chosen to explore and uncover the nature of their spiritual selves; they also still have a memory of their godliness.

Returning to the description you read earlier in this chapter, I want you to read these words slowly and allow whatever memory you can access to come alive with recognition as you digest that this is really you. You are going Home, you are flowing into the Mother Ocean, you are folding into the arms of your Creator.

> *The essence of you is infinitely loving, eternally peaceful, unconditionally allowing, eternally creative, graceful and gentle, kind, joyful, accepting, generous, honest, patient, fulfilled, trusting, calm, wise, childlike, open, connected, serene, complete, satisfied, whole and untroubled.*

That is your H^2O chemistry, and there's nothing you can do about it. You can never amend it or change it or alter it in any way. You can enhance the qualities of your physical life only by relating more to it, giving this part of you more authority over your thoughts and actions. However, it will continue to be what it has always been forever and ever throughout eternity. How does that make you feel? Do you have some awareness somewhere in some particle of your being that remembers this truth, as if waking from the memory of having been dreaming, knowing a dream was there, but not being able to say exactly what the dream was about?

What does this awareness do to your ego mind? Is it calmly accepting this truth? Is it rebelling, reacting, and throwing a tantrum, running away, getting reinforcements in the form of memories of previous sins? These messages from the ego are simply feeble attempts to convince you to stay in your beautiful wine glass. Those messages are all from the ego, or the glassware department. They can only serve to limit you from here on out.

Have you ever visited Niagara Falls, Victoria Falls, or some large waterfall? Have you witnessed how the water seems to run faster and stronger the closer it gets to the falls, whereas a few miles upstream it appears calm, and hapless canoers have no idea that a massive fall lies up ahead? Once you become more and more aware of your true nature, you will recognize a similar situation. You will want more of it, and you aren't prepared to wait any longer. Even if you are upstream somewhere, fishing and unaware of the fall that lies below, a pull begins towards the inevitable, and that inevitability is the truth of who you are.

And that is what the saying means, "The truth will set you free." It is the only truth that carries ultimate freedom—the knowing, not the perceiving, but the true knowing of who you essentially are. It isn't the believing, or the hearing, or the reading, but the experiential knowledge of your own Self.

This is freedom.

Epilogue

If you have found any part of this book helpful, I am delighted. However, my purpose was to create a manual for myself. I was looking for guidance in understanding *A Course in Miracles* and applying it in my life. I needed to write it down to refer to again and again. It helps to remind me exactly what I need to remember. Every example, every issue, every *you* was written explicitly for my own needs. Every quandary I encountered was resolved simply by asking, "What do I need to hear now?" And so I was guided.

That's the other part of this. It was all guided by my companion and internal voice of wisdom, Christ Consciousness or 'J' as I call him. This teacher is always patient and loving with me, invokes new thinking through simple questions that guide me to my own wisdom, as opposed to just feeding me his wisdom. Many of the sections are the results of a question followed by the resultant dialogue. Sometimes I related the conversations as best as I could remember, and other times I was the vehicle for words as I let my fingers type what inspiration sent. To corroborate the wisdom of my guidance is simply to feel its truth within. May you receive many blessings along your own spiritual journey. No doubt our paths will cross somewhere in our groggy state of Awakening.

Julie Hutslar

Resources

*I have had the esteemed privilege of working and collaborating with Julie for many years now. Julie's work and her books have been instrumental in the acceleration of my personal, spiritual and entrepreneurial growth. If you utilize her amazing talent and implement the knowledge gained by reading her books you will have the opportunity to fast forward through your negative beliefs, assisting you to achieve the life and lifestyle that you deserve. I wouldn't have the business success I've achieved today or have been able to create my book, **Cracking the Producer's Code**, if it weren't for the guidance and support I've received from Julie. Her unique approach of working from the inside out garners a completely different and more authentic result. I will incorporate Julie's work for the rest of my life.*

– Chad A Wade
Entrepreneur & Author of Cracking the Producer's Code

Core Belief Restructuring

At some point in your soul's journey, you begin to understand that the only thing that stands between you and your highest potential is your own perception. It may be manifesting as fear, anxiety, anger, hatred or simply self-sabotage, but it resides in the programming of the unconscious mind. When that realization occurs, you want to get it out; you begin to desire the release of all that prevents you from expressing your highest, most Divine Self. Core Belief Restructuring is one such avenue for releasing what currently stands in the way of you expressing that greatest potential.

A session in Core Belief Restructuring creates an opportunity to reprogram outdated beliefs that change the perceptions which have been limiting your reality. Using their own Divine Self as a blueprint, the client is given a rare opportunity to witness through their metaphysical self, the original or Divine Self which was created by the infinite creator of the universe. In observing and connecting with this Divine Self, assessments are made by the client's metaphysical self about which beliefs and thought processes need readjustment or simply releasing. During a session, the client makes the decision to release, through witnessing the power of creation, those individual perceptions that restrict the expression of one's highest potential. It is not about creating change, but about allowing for release which is infinitely more effortless than altering or tailoring. The goal is always to remove what stands between where you believe you are and all that you could be, or perhaps all that you already are, but simply do not recognize.

For more information, go to **www.jrhutslar.com**

Client Testimonials

"Julie has a unique ability to touch into places in me that I am scarcely aware of. She truly has the gift of empathy and a deep understanding of the depth of the human soul. She has inspired me to see myself with great compassion and understanding."
Kyle Mercer, President and Senior Teacher, The Garden Company

"Working with Julie on core beliefs is like opening an old suitcase you've been carrying around for years. Sorting through all those old things you've been hauling around with you, realizing they all served a purpose at one time or another, but now may no longer serve you then choosing the treasures you want to keep and take with you. This is what it was like for me. My suitcase is lighter and I'm happier and more peaceful."
Nita Mehlbrech, South Dakota

"My previous romantic relationships were usually abusive in some way because I thought that I had to prove to them that I was a good and worthy person. I thought that if they finally started treating me right then I had confirmation that I was good and worthy. Sounds insane right? As I was searching for a way to end this insane cycle, I met this wonderful man that challenged me in every way with my destructive beliefs by loving me unconditionally. I was confused because I didn't feel worthy of such wonderful treatment. After all, I didn't have to prove anything to him, he just loved me. About a month into the relationship I felt like I needed to schedule a session with Julie because of the confusion, doubts, and the low self-esteem I was experiencing. We worked together to release this baggage so that I could allow myself to have a healthy and truly loving relationship with my wonderful boyfriend, Jeremy. I appreciate Julie for all that she has done to help me remember who I really am and to help me recognize that I create experiences that are

love. After all, love is all that each of us can truly give one another."
Elizabeth Irene Adkinson, Utah

"I've always felt that things happened for a reason in your life, but it seemed that sometimes the "why" took an awful long time to reveal itself to me. The first session I had with Julie I can honestly say was one of the most amazing experiences I've had in my life, and each session thereafter has continued to bring meaning and understanding to things in my life in a way that touches something greater within myself. Each time we talk, I gain a great understanding of things that are happening in my life and why, and I can feel the shift in myself towards operating at a higher level of understanding and a greater awareness of myself and those around me. We're each carrying different baggage, or misconceptions, or coping mechanisms, or beliefs—whatever you want to call them—that manifest themselves at different times in our life and were created by some event in the past, and at some point we no longer need to hold to that belief anymore. The core of the work I have done with Julie has been in letting go of those things, and by doing so, it has opened more possibilities and ultimately I've gained a better understanding and happiness through that knowledge."
Kris K., Antarctica (yes, really, Antarctica)

"After a lifetime of confusion, fear and pain where nothing helped including religion, psychiatric care or drugs, I was lead to Julie who introduced me to her work. We have had many sessions together each one building, I believe, on the other. The last session in particular was a major breakthrough. Something huge rolled away. That is the only way I know how to describe it, like a huge boulder shifted and let me pass through to a place I have never been before. A real sense of being who I am supposed to be, who I was meant to be. Now there is lightness and laughter, a sense of well being. Until now I never thought I would be able to live up to the meaning of my name: Cindy—Bringer of Light."
Cindy Fischer, age 52, Arizona

"After my very first session I began to understand that I may be knocking my head against beliefs and patterns that no longer suited me in life. Once my eyes could see the truth, my energy shifted. I can honestly say that the only possible way that I have even had the genuine notion to unpack my baggage and move into my life is because of the impact that the core restructuring work has had on my very immediate emotional, physical, and karmic surroundings. This work has changed every part of how I see and has brought power and meaning to my work, relationships, and passion for the opportunity to learn about myself through life and relationships. The literal translation and metaphors that I have shown Julie have come into my life with great force especially in my creative life." *Stacie Webster, New York*

"Julie Hutslar's words have dispelled the night, and for me darkness is no more. She has gently guided me back to my true self by recognizing who I really am, and reflecting the glory, the love, the peace, the joy and the happiness back to me in a manner I could understand. The light of love has replaced the darkness of my hate." *Starla J. Adams, Washington*

"It has been my privilege to work with Julie for a number of years. Her intuitive insights and methods have guided me in the release of very old beliefs and led me to change long-standing patterns. As my level of understanding has increased it has been matched by an increased depth and breadth of focus on Julie's part. Each session with Julie helps me glimpse—a little more clearly each time—my own Divine template and my true Home." *Susan, Utah*

"I am so grateful for the insight and direction Julie Hutslar has offered me. When I first came to her I was living in an emotional space of fear and turmoil. Julie helped heal my soul from past experiences that I had interpreted negatively. I had formed misconceptions about universal laws and life. With Julie's help I was able to heal my spirit. Julie taught me how to refocus my energy. I am now able to tune into the loving power and direction that the universe offers. I have gained new perspective on life and I am now at peace in my life. Thank you Julie, I have such respect and adoration for the work you do." *Wendy McMillan, Utah*

"I began working with Julie and using the Core restructuring work only about a year ago. Though I have only had a few sessions, the impact of those has been immense as the visualization and symbolic imaging have allowed me to understand my metaphysical self in a more tangible way. I have taken these images and work and applied them to my physical life. The most striking example of this dealt with the image Julie relayed to me regarding how I deal with relationships. Images of harpooning a whale and then tagging along for the ride seemed to encompass much of my disgruntles in my own relationships. I was able to tangibly understand those images and as a result, make some profound changes in that part of my life." *Allie Beach, New York*

"There have been aspects to my personality that have frustrated me as I did not understand why I felt a certain way, or why I couldn't let go of something or someone. At times I have felt myself aching to let go of these frustrations and heartaches that I knew I was bringing on myself, but was unsure of how to help myself. I will never forget the first session I had with Julie, almost 5 years ago. I got her name and information from a dear friend and thought about it for months before I could set up an energy session. I was struggling through a very emotional time and finally felt so desperate for some kind of relief for my mind and heart that I decided to take a chance on her and her work. I can still remember the immense feeling of release, comprehension and forgiveness for myself and others that I felt that first day. I have since had several sessions and referred 3 of my close friends, all of which were truly in awe from the experience. I have learned so much about myself, others and about life from Julie and what she does, and will always be grateful and indebted—for there is no real way to repay that kind of caring and concern for others." *Jen Andrus, Nevada*

If you enjoyed *The Mask, the Mirror, and the Illusion*,
be sure to check out Julie's first book
(also available in audiobook):

Relationships: Gifts of the Spirit

How to view challenging relationships as opportunities for growth

In a time when we have more ways to communicate than ever before, greater ease of travel, and the most abundant information ever available, we still find ourselves struggling with the challenges of relationships, old as time itself. Whether with husband, wife, intimate other, boss, teenager, neighbor or parent, we often find ourselves in the midst of an emotionally ignited broil we can't figure out.

Many people spend a lifetime pointing the finger outside themselves, playing the victim card without positive results. Others flee negative relationships only to find themselves back in a very similar dynamic the next time around. Often we feel persecuted believing we are forced to be angry, or made to feel powerless, when quite possibly there is a different point of view we could take to unravel the relationship quandary.

Seeing through a different lens, the world looks different. This is how relationships need to evolve to be understood, defused and appreciated. The book, *Relationships: Gifts of the Spirit*, offers unique ways to look at and benefit from difficult relationships. Seen as teachers we have unconsciously selected, the challenging people in our lives represent important obstacles needed for our own personal growth. This book shows us the matrix in which relationships exist and why. Remove the word coincidence from your vocabulary to see all challenging experiences as opportunities to grow in ways we could never do alone. Find ways to understand why some of the most unlikely people show up in your life or why your parents or kids seem so unbearable. View life through the lens of responsibility and put the pointing finger down, then the doorway to self-discovery opens with remarkable clarity.

Book ordering information on last page.

Reader's Comments

"In *Relationships: Gifts of the Spirit*, Julie Hutslar draws upon her experiences and expertise with a form of energy healing she calls Accelerated Healing which she uses to assist others in locating and removing outdated, negative, and limiting beliefs to write a thoroughly "reader friendly" self-help manual for creating, exploring, developing, and re-developing personal, emotional, familial, and spiritual relationships. All worthwhile and long term relationships will have a degree of difficulty. Hutslar shows how to find ways to understand and benefit from those difficulties. Highly recommended and beneficial reading, *Relationships: Gifts of the Spirit* is an ideal and invaluable addition to any self-help, self-improvement, and relationship improvement reading list."
Midwest Book Review

"Your analogies are great–they really illuminate; and, you write like you speak–open, honest, telling it like it is, direct, with a lot of light and universal understanding. I am finding myself asking questions of the text and then having them answered by what I read next–interesting!"
Tanya Pankin, New York

"Reading Julie's book is like taking an awesome journey—it's like laying on the floor and having someone guide you through a meditation process and the end result—metamorphosis!"
Margaret Campbell, Utah

"After a deeply life altering divorce and the migration of my only child to 'greener pastures', *Relationships: Gifts of the Spirit* by Julie Hutslar has kept me company when I wake up alone. Her insight into the valuable lessons found at the heart of the most difficult relationships has also given me trust and faith in life, love and Spirit... when I find myself waking up with Mr. 'Maybe' who never was Mr. 'Right' or even Mr. 'Right Now'. Thank you, Julie, for your contribution to assisting the planet in achieving sanity."
Kathy Lowden, publisher, Voice of Choices Magazine

"I read some and have to put it down and then can't wait to pick it back up. What is wrong with me? Or has this been a normal response when people read your book? I feel... actually I am struggling to put a word to the feeling. I relate to so much it feels kind of scary. Oh I don't know... should I just keep reading? I found as I was reading that it was very difficult to read the last chapter. To love myself is hard. The whole thing about my soul being good has helped so much... oh my gosh, I could just go on and on and on. I'm almost done with your book so you better hurry and write another one, when all felt lost yesterday I started reading and found some hope. Thank you Julie. I am starting to believe that I might even deserve to feel the spark of joy that is touching my heart right here right now."
Emily Barrett, Utah

"This book helped me see how I view my intimate relationships through the ego or the eyes of fear. Neither one of these will lead to a successful relationship. I was able to safely extricate myself for a moment from these inhibitors and view my fellow human beings with my heart. It was a profound moment, that brought me to tears. I hope to be able to continue to have these moments more and more often. I will forever be indebted to Ms. Hutslar for sharing her insights."
Mary Trost, California

"I had a great time reading a text written by an author that has a writing style that feels like a conversation rather than a book. Her issues are to the point and written with an elegant ease that enables a "regular" guy to understand without a dictionary or 10 years of study. Ms. Hutslar perfectly described and explained my relationship with my wife (which is not a simple one). Oddly enough, it is the same relationship she has with her husband. Her explanation of her relationship and the way it manifests and works for her is an excellent blueprint that you can try for yourself. In summary, it was a great and easy read with many useful insights. I highly recommend it for men and women who are "lost in space" trying to find a practical relationship concept to anchor your mature thinking." *Jeff Stephanina, Virginia*

"I cannot but bow to your courageous, candid and compassionate writing that transformed a rather mundane, overworked subject of relationships into a deeply 'no stones left unturned' probing yet refreshingly liberating book, for those brave hearts that are willing to look at all their relationships square in the eyes and know with all certainty, each one was of their own choosing, for better or worse, and each one offered a unique opportunity, acted upon or not, to glow a little brighter in the light of divine love. Thank you for gently reminding me that my husband's self-destructive and addictive tendencies are his own 'stuff', not mine – his carefully chosen personal baggage to grow through just as my 'never good enough' core belief and perfectionist, 'control freak' propensities are my selected earth issues to hopefully overcome in less than nine lifetimes." *Jennifer Taylor, British Columbia*

"You are, in the very best sense, unbelievable, but believe I do! Listening to your initial chapters on CD while driving to and from an event, I felt as if you were totally present and so accessible! Your husband ("–" polarity with such a fine balance) emerges as a complex and gifted man who happens to have an utterly unique ("+" polarity) partner and the two of you together perfectly illustrate Buddhist non-duality. Listening to you talk on CD (you "read" your text so wonderfully well, it's hard to believe you're not just conversing) is the next best thing to hearing you in person. WOW!!!" *Virginia Lohner, Illinois*

"Not a Self Help book, this is a Heal Thyself book. In a gentle, caring, and lighthearted voice, Ms. Hutslar shines a light on the mysteries of our everyday relationships. To welcome the concept of these relationships as special gifts (especially the challenging ones!) is a miraculous eye opener! I turned from page to page, as if I was reading a letter written to me personally by my best friend. Once finished with the book myself, I have talked about it and shuttled it lovingly from friend, to family, to co-worker (I have an extra copy I keep safely at home!). This book is a gift you deserve to give yourself." *Laura Sheridan, California*

Book Orders

Books by Julie Hutslar may be purchased through your local book store, through on-line merchants such as www.amazon.com, or from the author.

If you would like a signed copy, go directly to the author's web site at **www.jrhutslar.com**, or send a check to the publisher at:

Luminous Epinoia Press
P.O. Box 2547
Sandpoint, ID 83864
(800) 786-1090

The Mask, the Mirror, and the Illusion
© 2008 by Julie Hutslar
Luminous Epinoia Press
ISBN: 978-0-9753000-0-8
USA $15.00

Relationships: Gifts of the Spirit
© 2004 by Julie Hutslar
Luminous Epinoia Press
ISBN: 978-0-9753000-4-6
USA $15.00

Relationships: Gifts of the Spirit–Audiobook
7 CD audiobook with bonus CD that includes entire e-book.
© 2008 by Julie Hutslar
Luminous Epinoia Press
ISBN: 978-0-9753000-6-0
USA $28.00